ADVANCE PRAISE

"In *Help for the Helper Workbook*, Babette Rothschild and Vanessa Bear offer a vital resource for all helping professionals. Through practical exercises and evidence-based strategies, readers learn to manage empathy, regulate their nervous system, and prioritize self-care—making it essential for therapists, first responders, and caregivers seeking sustainable well-being in demanding fields."

—**Linda A. Curran, BCPC, LPC,** international trainer, author of
Trauma Competency and *101 Trauma-Informed Interventions*

"Therapist self-care is an important topic in the helping professions at a time when many are experiencing the very real threat of compassion fatigue and burnout. The *Help for the Helper Workbook* is the best medicine for this I have seen yet: It is a well-constructed and comprehensive self-help course which will leave its graduates not only with refreshed passion for their work, but also with just the right toolkit for keeping themselves sane, healthy and in good spirits for a long time to come."

—**Kathrin A. Stauffer, PhD,** psychotherapist,
author of *Emotional Neglect and the Adult in Therapy*

HELP FOR THE *HELPER* WORKBOOK

HELP FOR THE *HELPER* WORKBOOK

Personalize Your Toolkit to Prevent Compassion Fatigue and Vicarious Trauma

Babette Rothschild

Vanessa Bear

Norton Professional Books

An Imprint of W. W. Norton & Company
Independent Publishers Since 1923

This book is intended as a general information resource for professionals practicing in the field of psychotherapy and mental health, as well as practitioners in other helping professions, including, but not limited to, doctors, nurses, emergency workers, first responders, and massage therapists and other body work practitioners. It is not a substitute for appropriate training or clinical supervision. Standards of clinical practice and protocol change over time. No technique or recommendation is guaranteed to be safe or effective in all circumstances, and neither the publisher nor the authors can guarantee the complete accuracy, efficacy, or appropriateness of any particular recommendation in every respect.

If you have any physical limitations, please consult your healthcare provider before attempting the physical exercises described in this book and follow the instructions given for each exercise carefully, since even simple stretching can cause injuries if it is performed incorrectly or inappropriately.

All the therapists and patients described in this book, and all session transcripts, are composites. Any URLs displayed in this book link or refer to websites that existed as of press time. The publisher is not responsible for, and should not be deemed to endorse or recommend, any website, app, or other content that it did not create. The authors, also, are not responsible for any third-party material.

For information about permission to reproduce selections from this book, write to Permissions, W. W. Norton & Company, Inc., 500 Fifth Avenue, New York, NY 10110

For information about special discounts for bulk purchases, please contact W. W. Norton Special Sales at specialsales@wwnorton.com or 800-233-4830

Manufacturing by Versa Press
Book design by Chrissy Kurpeski
Production manager: Gwen Cullen

Library of Congress Cataloging-in-Publication Data
Names: Rothschild, Babette author | Bear, Vanessa author
Title: Help for the helper workbook : personalize your toolkit to prevent   compassion fatigue and vicarious trauma / Babette Rothschild and Vanessa Bear.
Description: First edition. | New York, NY : Norton Professional Books, [2026] | Includes bibliographical references and index.
Identifiers: LCCN 2025054806 | ISBN 9781324053682 paperback | ISBN 9781324083979 ebook
Subjects: LCSH: Secondary traumatic stress--Treatment | Psychotherapists--Job stress | Mental health personnel--Mental health | Emergency medical personnel--Job stress | Caregivers--Mental health
Classification: LCC RC552.P67 R6857 2026
LC record available at https://lccn.loc.gov/2025054806

W. W. Norton & Company, Inc., 500 Fifth Avenue, New York, NY 10110
www.wwnorton.com

W. W. Norton & Company Ltd., 15 Carlisle Street, London W1D 3BS

Authorized EU representative: EAS, Mustamäe tee 50, 10621 Tallinn, Estonia

1 2 3 4 5 6 7 8 9 0

*For all those, especially the helpers, who
strive to make the world safer and happier.*

*For all who have taught, encouraged, and supported us
and for Mother Nature, whose nourishment sustains us.*

Contents

Acknowledgments

We would like to thank each other, Vanessa and Babette, for the genuinely wonderful, warm, good-humored, and supportive experience of writing this workbook together.

Many thanks to Sam Bear and Alex Jenkins, who took the time to read drafts, offer suggestions, and help us catch spelling and grammatical errors we might otherwise have missed. We are very grateful for your care and attention. We really appreciate and value you.

With deep gratitude for all the helping professionals who have inspired this workbook. We truly hope that it is useful.

Thanks to our brilliant and supportive editor, Deborah Malmud, and to McKenna Tanner, who generously went above and beyond in supporting us during the publishing process. Thanks so much to Olivia, Mariah, Jamie, Kevin, Talya, Joy, and the whole team at Norton for supporting us through our second publication together.

Introduction

You probably know a range of quotes, idioms, and metaphors related to the importance of taking care of yourself before you take care of someone else. You possibly even share them regularly with clients, supervisees, and family members. These might include sayings such as "You can't pour from an empty cup," "Put your own oxygen mask on first," and the quote, "Compassionate toward yourself, you reconcile all beings in the world" (Tzu, 1996). However, many find it difficult to practice what they preach, to prioritize their own needs.

The culture of the helping profession can contribute to this difficulty. Few therapists experience any time devoted to self-care as part of their training. Rather, many are told to completely ignore their own needs and prioritize those of the person they are helping. In this workbook we* shall explore why we believe this is not useful and could possibly be dangerous for both therapists and their clients. Exercises are provided to help develop the self-care strategies we believe are essential to long-term health, well-being, and effective care of others.

Research has shown that therapist self-compassion can prevent burnout (Richardson et al., 2020), compassion fatigue, and secondary traumatization (Crego et al., 2022) as well as increasing compassion for others (Miller & Kelly, 2020). Many colleagues have shared that there is an assumption among their friends that a therapist must "have it all together," that, unlike all other human beings, they should not be affected by grief, stress, or tiredness, or succumb to emotional distress. This myth can be carried into the profession, so that therapists feel ashamed of these normal human experiences, to the point where many feel reluctant to get support because they "should know better" or "they aren't good therapists if they can't help themselves." Most do not realize that seeking support, through a workbook or a therapist or supervision, will actually enhance the value of what their work provides for others.

Working with people in emotional distress can be challenging. The phrase "wounded healers," coined by Carl Jung, is commonly used for therapists. Many have

---

* Throughout this book "we" will refer to the two authors, Babette and Vanessa.

come to the helping professions after working through many of their own life challenges. However, no matter how many hours of therapy you may have had, in times of stress those who have experienced trauma may have increased vulnerability. Of course, working with a client who has experienced a difficulty similar to one of your own can provide you with insight and possibly greater understanding. However, it can also be triggering.

The most important tool for your own self-care is awareness. Developing a keen knowledge of your strengths and weaknesses, your needs, what supports you, and what doesn't, can help you to avoid burnout, compassion fatigue, and vicarious traumatization. It is our hope that this workbook will be invaluable for your own well-being and the well-being of your clients.

THE WORKBOOK

This workbook was written following publication of the second edition of *Help for the Helper*, written by Babette Rothschild. The first edition was published by W. W. Norton in 2006. That book focuses more on theory with exercises peppered throughout. In mirror image, this workbook's focus is on exercises with theory sprinkled in. While either book will be helpful on its own, the two are a set that complement each other. We have kept to the same chapter headings so that you can refer to each book with greater ease, to get a little more theory from the original or a little more practical resource from this workbook.

We will refer to ourselves in the workbook now and then, sharing our personal experience. When we do so, we will simply use our names, Vanessa and/or Babette.

MAKE IT YOURS

The tools, strategies, and exercises in this workbook have all been taken from those we have shared successfully with clients or have been useful to ourselves and our supervisees, colleagues, and friends. However, no exercise, strategy, or tool is useful for everyone all the time. Please be discerning. Notice what is and what is not useful to you. You will likely need to adapt many of the exercises to best suit your personal needs and circumstances. Experiment to find what is useful for you, adapting or rejecting any as you see fit. Personalize a toolkit that is exactly right for you.

Although none of the exercises herein are meant to be triggering or distressing, it is impossible to completely avoid any possibility of that. If you notice an adverse reaction to any theory, instruction, tool, or exercise, stop! Please do not suffer through any content that is distressing or not helpful for you.

We suggest that you distinguish between your own self-care and what might be useful for your clients while working through this book, even if strategies might be similar. Vanessa learned the value of this when she first became a yoga teacher. She found attending yoga classes much less enjoyable and less personally useful when she was thinking about how she might use or adapt what the teacher was sharing with her own students. Rather than leaving the class feeling strong in her body and peaceful in her mind, she noticed that she had been so distracted that she had not taken much care of her body and still had a busy mind. It took some practice, but she eventually learned to use personal yoga classes for herself and training workshops for her clients.

Similarly, you may find yourself thinking about your clients while reading this book, noticing that a particular exercise might be useful for them rather than focusing on your own needs. Likely, some of the exercises may indeed be useful to some of your clients. Perhaps make a note of that and then turn your attention back to yourself. Simply noticing that your attention has wandered from yourself may be useful in bringing yourself back into focus on you. Then, when you are spending time specifically intended to be spent on your clients, you can refer to your notes or return to this book and find exercises that you think will be useful for them.

We encourage you to use this workbook in a way that best suits you. Personalize it. For those of you with a paper copy, you might like to write in the spaces we have made in the workbook itself, or you may prefer to have a journal that you write in. Those of you with an electronic version will likely need a journal, whether paper based or electronic. You may decide to read through the whole book before starting any of the exercises, or you may start at the beginning and work your way straight through. You could also decide to look through the contents page and go to exercises and sections that most interest you on that day. There is no right or wrong strategy, and we encourage you to follow the path best suited to your own needs and ways of working.

MAKE TIME

Working through this workbook will be a commitment that you will be adding to your likely already busy life. However, you will need to set time aside to do it in order to get the most out of it. Be realistic with the amount of time you set aside in your day to work through it so that self-care does not add stress. Think of *The Tortoise and the Hare*: A small amount done regularly will get you farther than a large amount done irregularly.

TERMINOLOGY

We have intended to use words that promote inclusiveness in this workbook. However, we are aware that terminology differs and changes according to place and time. We apologize for any that cause distress, as well as for any omission. None are intentional.

DISCLAIMER

The exercises shared in this workbook are based on our experience of what has been useful to colleagues, supervisees, and friends. The theory we refer to is generally accepted and current at the moment we wrote it. However, theory is just that, and as such is forever evolving as we continue to learn and understand more about the brain and about relationships and connections. As such, it is important that you employ your own common sense as well as your own gauge to determine what is and is not useful to you.

HELP FOR THE *HELPER* WORKBOOK

CHAPTER 1

Psychotherapists at Risk

Reducing your risk of being negatively impacted by your work as a psychotherapist or other helping professional is the aim of this workbook. The first step toward that goal is understanding what exactly those risks might be. This chapter will help you to identify and begin to explore your possible risks, beginning with the foundational phenomena of empathy and emotional contagion, and then going on to the more recognized risks of compassion fatigue, vicarious traumatization, burnout, and unmanaged countertransference.

EMPATHY AND EMOTIONAL CONTAGION

Sofia's client, Lizzie, arrived at her session late and agitated. She told Sofia that she felt panicked as she had just seen someone who reminded her of her past attacker. Though she had felt scared, she said that she had known it was not him, as she had been able to stay calm enough to take a really good look. However, it had rattled her, and she had gone into a store to wait until she was sure he was gone.

Observing that Lizzie was still visibly shaking and breathing quickly, Sofia noticed her own heartbeat had increased and that she, too, was feeling a little panicked. Sofia invited Lizzie to do some of the grounding and calming exercises that they had done in the past for stabilization. Those helped Lizzie to stop shaking, and after a little while she felt calmer. In sync, Sofia also noticed that her own heartbeat had steadied and that the calming exercises had helped her to feel more grounded as well.

After the session, Sofia noticed that despite feeling much calmer than she had when Lizzie first arrived, she still felt a little shaken up.

What might have caused Sofia to feel as panicked as Lizzie? The answer lies in understanding the phenomenon of empathy. Empathy enables a person to feel what another person is feeling. Whether it is conscious or unconscious, empathy makes it possible to "walk in the other person's shoes," so to speak, for a longer or shorter period of time. When empathy is conscious and brief, it can be an exceedingly useful and valuable therapeutic tool. However, if it is happening unconsciously, unbeknownst to the therapist, or goes on for an extended period of time, the risk to a therapist of being negatively impacted can sometimes have serious consequences. That is likely what happened to Sofia.

Emotional contagion is one of the common consequences of empathy. Simply put, emotional contagion means just what it says: being infected by another's emotions, just as you can be infected by influenza or COVID-19. On one end of the emotional spectrum, it can look like family around the dinner table all dissolving into laughter because a toddler has begun to giggle uncontrollably. On the other end of the spectrum, a child can become scared to do something because of their parent's fear of the same thing. In the therapy room, a therapist might share in the happiness of a client's accomplishment or, on the other hand, could start to feel, and be impaired by, the hopelessness their client comes in with.

Chapter 2 is devoted to expanding your understanding of empathy and gaining tools to minimize the risks, such as Sofia's experience. For now, with regard to evaluating your own risk factors, it might be useful to just observe. You can start by gradually increasing your awareness of your own emotional and physical reactions when you are with clients and in the moments after a client leaves. Notice where there are parallels and jot them down below.

_____

_____

_____

_____

_____

_____

_____

_____

_____

_____

DEFINING THE RECOGNIZED RISKS

Compassion Fatigue

> **Definition:** Emotional and/or physical exhaustion from engaging in compassionate work. It is most likely to occur when you prioritize others' well-being over your own.

> *Meera works full time as a psychotherapist. Her client base is predominantly made up of young women who have experienced sexual assault. Meera is deeply committed to her work: She often stays late to write up notes and regularly skips lunch so that she can run an additional group session. She rarely takes her annual vacation time as she is worried that her clients may be at risk without the sessions. Meera often feels exhausted and as though she is on autopilot.*

Compassion fatigue is a term first coined by Charles Figley (2002), who described it as "a state experienced by those helping people or animals in distress; it is an extreme state of tension and preoccupation with the suffering of those being helped to the degree that it can lead to secondary traumatic stress for the helper" (p. 1435).

Usually, compassion fatigue can be managed by developing awareness and balance between personal and work life. However, due to the nature of compassion fatigue, for those who tend to put others' well-being before their own at home as well as at work, the risk is higher. This might be due to a habit of people-pleasing or living up to a label of being the caring one, or it might be due to practical limitations, such as an agency being short staffed, or caring for an ill family member. Whatever the reason, if you consistently prioritize care of others over care of yourself, then your well-being will suffer. In actuality, caring for others effectively and over the long term requires a strength that can only be sustained by someone who prioritizes their own self-care.

It is likely that Meera is already suffering the consequences of compassion fatigue, indicated by her feeling that she's on autopilot. For those who have been taught from a young age that kindness means always putting others first, it can be difficult to accept that prioritizing your own well-being could be necessary to sustain your ability to do the work you love. For daily well-being, a good model to remember is provided by common airline safety and emergency instructions that are usually presented at the beginning of each flight. Every airline advises that in an emergency, you should *put your own oxygen mask on first, before helping others.* That protects not only yourself but also others you might hope to help. Think about it: If you put on another's mask first and then succumb to a lack of oxygen yourself, you will not be able to assist anyone else. In the same way, prioritizing your own well-being in your life ensures that you have the capacity to assist your clients, as well as yourself, and your family.

Exercises for Preventing Compassion Fatigue

The exercises below are designed to raise your awareness of how much you may be at risk of compassion fatigue. Many of them ask you to estimate a percentage of your energy that is in use. There is no wrong answer; just estimate as close as possible. And if you do not relate to the idea of percentages, then feel free to substitute your own gauge, for example: a lot, a little, not much, or not at all.

EXERCISE Self-Care Check-In

It can be useful to regularly check whether you are succeeding with or neglecting your self-care. Below, put a check next to any of the following statements that applied to you within the last couple of weeks. Next to each one you check, write a brief example of what happened.

For example:

☑ Pushed aside your own feelings to prioritize those of others.
Last Wednesday, even though I needed to get home, I did not want to interrupt a distressed client. The session ran overtime. After that session, I felt exhausted and wanted to go straight home, but I needed to stay later to write the session notes.

☐ Pushed aside your own feelings to prioritize those of others

_____

_____

☐ Isolated yourself, and didn't seek support for yourself

_____

_____

☐ Increased alcohol intake

_____

_____

☐ Decreased physical well-being

_____

_____

☐ Increased illness or reduced immunity

_____

_____

☐ Skipped meals or appetite changed

_____

_____

☐ Neglected hydration

_____

_____

☐ Reduced or avoided breaks and rest periods

_____

_____

☐ Postponed normal time off such as evenings, weekends, or holidays

_____

_____

☐ Felt guilty about taking any time out for yourself

_____

_____

☐ Worked beyond the hours you are actually paid for

_____

_____

☐ Delayed or stopped taking vacation time

_____

_____

EXERCISE   Showing Yourself Compassion

Showing the same compassion for yourself as you do for others might be difficult. It can help to imagine compassionately advising someone else who is in a similar situation. In the space below, write down what you would advise a close friend or colleague if they told you they were overworking to the point of exhaustion.

_____

_____

_____

_____

_____

_____

EXERCISE   Monitor Your Energy Levels

Meera's workdays are filled with looking after other people who are experiencing powerful emotions. The likelihood of emotional contagion due to being on autopilot is high, and Meera has not prioritized any time for herself. When a friend invited her for dinner recently, she declined because she needed to catch up on laundry and other household chores. However, she felt very sad to have missed a chance for contact, relaxation, and enjoyment. She often feels overwhelmed and helpless and has trouble sleeping.

It is never a good idea to deplete your entire energy level; keeping some in reserve is important. Developing awareness of your energy levels at different times of the day, while doing various tasks and working with different types of clients, could help you stay in control and avoid fatigue.

1. In the table below, track your energy level for one week. Notice and record it at different times of the day. Shade in the energy level bar from 0% to 100%, with 0% meaning that you have expended all of your energy and are

extremely tired, and 100% meaning that you are well rested with plenty of energy to spare.

Day	Morning	Afternoon	Evening
Example	0% ▭▭▭▭▭▭▭ 100%	0% ▭▭▭▭ 100%	0% ▭▭▭▭▭▭▭ 100%
Monday	0% ▭▭▭▭▭▭▭▭ 100%	0% ▭▭▭▭▭▭▭▭ 100%	0% ▭▭▭▭▭▭▭▭ 100%
Tuesday	0% ▭▭▭▭▭▭▭▭ 100%	0% ▭▭▭▭▭▭▭▭ 100%	0% ▭▭▭▭▭▭▭▭ 100%
Wednesday	0% ▭▭▭▭▭▭▭▭ 100%	0% ▭▭▭▭▭▭▭▭ 100%	0% ▭▭▭▭▭▭▭▭ 100%
Thursday	0% ▭▭▭▭▭▭▭▭ 100%	0% ▭▭▭▭▭▭▭▭ 100%	0% ▭▭▭▭▭▭▭▭ 100%
Friday	0% ▭▭▭▭▭▭▭▭ 100%	0% ▭▭▭▭▭▭▭▭ 100%	0% ▭▭▭▭▭▭▭▭ 100%
Saturday	0% ▭▭▭▭▭▭▭▭ 100%	0% ▭▭▭▭▭▭▭▭ 100%	0% ▭▭▭▭▭▭▭▭ 100%
Sunday	0% ▭▭▭▭▭▭▭▭ 100%	0% ▭▭▭▭▭▭▭▭ 100%	0% ▭▭▭▭▭▭▭▭ 100%

2. Consider the activities you do throughout the day at work, including in-person sessions, online sessions, supervision, meetings, paperwork, making telephone calls, and so on. Then consider activities outside of work, particularly those that involve caregiving for family or friends. For each of these activities, gauge how much energy you have before and after the activity; this will give some indication of the amount of energy that you are expending on the activity. You might want to include specific clients.

Meera realized that she had appointments with all of her clients who were in crisis on Mondays, which often left her so tired that the rest of her week was compromised. She decided to ask some of her clients to change their appointment time so that she could spread their exceptional stress throughout the week. Although she was concerned about broaching this, she found that most were happy to comply with her request. She also made a point to take client stresses into consideration when scheduling new clients to continue to better balance her week.

Activity	Energy before	Energy after	Day of the week	Time of day usually completed
Dropping kids at school	0% 100%	0% 100%	*Monday - Friday*	*Morning*
Three back-to-back clients	0% 100%	0% 100%	*Wednesday*	*Afternoon*
	0% 100%	0% 100%		
	0% 100%	0% 100%		
	0% 100%	0% 100%		
	0% 100%	0% 100%		
	0% 100%	0% 100%		
	0% 100%	0% 100%		
	0% 100%	0% 100%		
	0% 100%	0% 100%		
	0% 100%	0% 100%		
	0% 100%	0% 100%		

3. Reflect on the table from Part 2 above and take some time to consider how it might be possible to move tasks and particular clients to different days of the week or within a particular day to optimize your available energy.

_____

_____

4. If you find yourself not wanting to disrupt your or your client's routine, write in the space below what you would advise a colleague who worried about moving things around to better preserve their own energy needs.

_____

_____

_____

_____

_____

_____

_____

_____

EXERCISE   Finding Nourishment

When Meera's friend invited her for dinner, Meera chose not to go, as she prioritized catching up on laundry. However, later she realized such time spent with a good friend could have offered her some respite. Many therapists and other helpers put aside nourishing opportunities due to being too busy or feeling exhausted. However, often opportunities such as spending time with friends, or even exercising, can actually boost energy levels and offer the respite and nourishment essential to well-being.

1. How else can you keep your energy account "in the black"? Consider each of the suggestions below. Tick any that you will try, and make a date with yourself to try them. There is also space for you to write other ways you can support your energy levels.

   ☐ Eat foods that boost my energy

   ☐ Drink plenty of hydrating liquids including water

   ☐ Fit manageable doses of exercise into my day, for example, parking a little further away or going for a walk at lunchtime

   ☐ Take mini relaxation breaks throughout the day, such as looking out the window or doing a mindfulness exercise

   ☐ Explore ways to "switch off" from work when not at work (we will explore these in Chapter 5)

□ Spend time with friends

□ Read novels

□ Sing with a choir

□ Walk in nature

□ Go for a bike ride

□ Walk the dog

□ Spend time with my partner

□ Visit a local park

□ Work out at the gym

□ Listen to music

□ Dance

□ Take a nap

□ Watch a favorite movie or series

□ _____

□ _____

2. In the table below, track your energy levels before, during, and after the activity.

Activity	Energy before		Energy during		Energy after	
	0% 100%		0% 100%		0% 100%	
	0% 100%		0% 100%		0% 100%	
	0% 100%		0% 100%		0% 100%	
	0% 100%		0% 100%		0% 100%	
	0% 100%		0% 100%		0% 100%	
	0% 100%		0% 100%		0% 100%	
	0% 100%		0% 100%		0% 100%	
	0% 100%		0% 100%		0% 100%	
	0% 100%		0% 100%		0% 100%	

EXERCISE Evaluate How Foods Affect Your Energy Levels

Many dieticians identify particular foods that affect our mood and energy levels. For example, while sugar and caffeine can give us a quick hit of energy, people generally find that they cause a greater energy slump later in the day. Complex carbohydrates, such as oatmeal, bananas, broccoli, and apples, along with proteins and healthy fats such as sunflower seeds and nuts, can usually supply longer lasting energy.

While there are broad suggestions, there can be individual differences. You may notice patterns of foods that affect you more or less than others.

1. In the chart below, for a week, make a note of everything you eat.
2. Add a description of your energy level, such as "lethargic," "energized," or "restless."

   Please use caution and get advice from a professional before doing this exercise if you have a history of disordered eating.

		What you ate	Energy level
Monday	Morning		0% 100%
	Afternoon		0% 100%
	Evening		0% 100%
Tuesday	Morning		0% 100%
	Afternoon		0% 100%
	Evening		0% 100%
Wednesday	Morning		0% 100%
	Afternoon		0% 100%
	Evening		0% 100%

		What you ate	**Energy level**
Thursday	Morning		0% 100%
	Afternoon		0% 100%
	Evening		0% 100%
Friday	Morning		0% 100%
	Afternoon		0% 100%
	Evening		0% 100%
Saturday	Morning		0% 100%
	Afternoon		0% 100%
	Evening		0% 100%
Sunday	Morning		0% 100%
	Afternoon		0% 100%
	Evening		0% 100%

3. In the table above, choose a different color to highlight the foods that you notice:
   - Make you feel full of energy but then cause fatigue later
   - Tend to enable you to have long-lasting energy
   - Tend to make you feel depleted in energy
4. Notice whether there are any other patterns affecting your energy levels, such as the time of day you do or do not eat. Note them below.

_____

_____

_____

_____

EXERCISE Combining Nourishing Activities

Meera wondered whether it would be possible to combine watching her daughter with a visit to the community garden (her favorite place to feel calm) while also spending time with the friend who had invited her for dinner. She had not thought her friend would want to visit the community garden and that she might be too distracted by her daughter to spend quality time with her friend. However, her friend was happy to meet in the garden. Though the friend is not so keen on gardening, she wanted to see the place that Meera enjoyed so much. Her friend also suggested bringing her own niece along for Meera's daughter to play with. While the children were playing, Meera and her friend had time to catch up too. Since that arrangement worked out, it reminded Meera that a little creativity could go a long way, particularly if she shared her concerns or limitations with a friend who could contribute to the problem solving.

1. Could any of the nourishing activities from the Finding Nourishment exercise above be combined easily into your timetable to have even more positive impact? *For example, walking the dog in your favorite park or cycling home from work with your partner.*

_____

_____

_____

_____

Meera had not really prioritized seeing her friend and had not expected her to want to come to the community garden. She had also forgotten how important being in that place was to her. But the day after that visit she felt more nourished and rested than she had in a long time, as though she had had a mini holiday. That success helped her to remember the value of such activities and the importance of including them in her schedule. Meera and her friend decided to do the same every other week.

2. Read back through the nourishing activities you have written about in the previous exercises. Choose one to include in your schedule for next week. Allocate a

set amount of time and set an alarm to remind you. Notice and jot down how you feel before and after in the space below.

Activity:

_____

Date and time:

_____

Feelings before:

_____

_____

Feelings immediately afterward:

_____

_____

Feelings the next day:

_____

_____

3. Once you have added nourishing activities to your schedule, assess the impact by doing the Monitor Your Energy Levels exercise again and see if it would be useful to amend which activities you do or when you do them.

EXERCISE Mini Nourishment

Meera often felt better after a walk outdoors, moving her body and spending time in nature. She decided that when she did not have time for a long walk at lunchtime, she would just walk once around the block, or even take a short walk along the corridor of her building and then spend a few minutes looking out of an open window, feeling the breeze on her face.

Meera also remembered that she had enjoyed watching birds as a child. Her grandmother always had a full bird feeder, and birds would flock to her yard. She decided to take a few minutes between clients to watch for birds outside her office window. Eventually she bought a bird feeder and set it where she could see it between clients.

> *Meera decided to keep a photograph of herself at the community garden with her daughter and friend on her desk. She took time to look at it now and then and remember being there. When she did, she noticed feeling warm, calm, and happy.*

What additional small activities could you fit into your schedule that nourish you? For example, listening to a favorite song in between clients, taking a short walk around the block, a 5-minute meditation, watching birds out the window, a short nap after lunch, eating lunch at a nearby park.

_____

_____

_____

Vicarious Trauma

Definition: Experiencing a response or symptoms that resemble post-traumatic stress disorder (PTSD), such as nightmares, physical symptoms, or intrusive images, that mirror those of one or more of your clients, without roots in your own history. For example, having intrusive images and unusual fears of being assaulted like your client when that has never happened to you. Trauma therapists are particularly vulnerable to vicarious trauma, though being infected by another's trauma can happen to anyone.

> *Gabriela came to supervision describing how one of her clients had recently shared their experience of domestic abuse. Despite domestic abuse not being part of her own history, Gabriela had started to have violent nightmares and was experiencing problems in her relationship, including feeling increasingly on edge around her gentle and loving partner.*
>
> *Gabriela described how, during the client sessions, she imagined the things that her client told her, and often saw her client's situation in her mind's eye as if it were happening to herself. Sometimes those images came to her unbidden. However, at times Gabriela purposely created them because she believed that doing so might give her more understanding and empathy for her client who was experiencing something that she had not. Her supervisor helped her to realize that this practice was likely causing the problems she was experiencing, and that*

her client would benefit more from a therapist who was able to stay calm and present than one whose nervous system was similarly overwhelmed.

Using mindful awareness as she had practiced it in supervision, Gabriela paid attention in sessions to catch when she was imagining the trauma stories she was told, particularly when imagining they could happen to her. Over time, her increased awareness made it possible for her to intentionally stop the images. In addition, when she woke from a nightmare or felt nervous around her partner, she reminded herself that she was remembering the story that her client had told her, which, gratefully, had not happened to her. Using those tools, the symptoms she had been experiencing subsided.

Just as we discussed emotions being contagious earlier in this chapter, as Gabriela's situation illustrates, trauma too can be contagious. Vicarious trauma can occur when someone who listens to stories about another's trauma overidentifies with that person's story. Vicarious trauma causes symptoms in the listener as if the trauma had actually happened to them.

It is important to note that vicarious trauma is different from the traumatization that can occur from witnessing trauma firsthand, which would be classed in the *Diagnostic and Statistical Manual of Mental Disorders* as primary trauma. For example, those of you who work as first responders may be likely to experience primary traumatization from being a witness at the scene of an accident, while a psychotherapist who is told about a client's accident may experience vicarious trauma.

Identification with the experiences of others happens frequently and is often not problematic. People watching a soccer match can be observed to make micro movements of their bodies as they watch the players weave down the pitch, as though they were playing too. They groan with the same sense of loss as the player who misses a shot. Likewise, when you listen to clients describing incidents that have befallen them, identifying with their trauma can cause your nervous systems to react in the same way as theirs.

The risk of overidentification usually comes via empathy in the form of putting yourself in the shoes of a client. For example, when a client is talking about a traumatic event, you might imagine what it would have been like if it happened to you and picture the event in first person. Your self-talk may also include the possibility that what happened to your client could have happened to you. These might be more likely if you have a history similar to that of your client, as it may be even easier to imagine yourself being in their shoes.

Putting yourself in your clients' shoes may seem like a useful thing to do at first.

Children are often told to do this to help them develop empathy and compassion for others. However, like Gabriela and her client, when working with someone caught in a whirlpool of distress, there can be risk to both client and therapist. The client will benefit more from a present, grounded, and steady therapist who stands at the shore to throw them a lifeline than a therapist who jumps into the whirlpool with them. Exercises in the following chapters will explore a variety of tools that can help therapists to stay present and grounded.

Sharing your feelings with colleagues is one way to be supported, and at times sharing information about a client may be necessary, such as where there is a safeguarding concern or within a multidisciplinary team supporting a client. Yet it may be important to notice what and how the information is shared. In the book *The Cat in the Hat Comes Back* by Dr. Seuss, a pink stain appears around the tub when the cat has a bath. The stain is quickly transferred to almost everything in the house and even to the snow outside. That is just like vicarious trauma. To avoid passing vicarious trauma further on to your colleagues, it may be appropriate to give them fair warning before sharing any potentially distressing details, or to consider which details are necessary to share and hold back those that are not.

If you are a clinical supervisor, it can be useful to set a ground rule with supervisees that they state a warning before they tell you details of a traumatic incident. If you are a supervisee, this may also be useful for you, as an overwhelmed or triggered supervisor is unlikely to be able to offer useful insights. This can be as simple as letting the supervisor know that you would like to share the details of something you were told. That way the supervisor has time to put strategies in place to shore up their boundaries and stay grounded. It also gives the supervisor a choice about whether or not this is a good time to hear such a thing or to help the supervisee sort which details are most relevant. If the supervisee shares the title or summary of the situation, it will give an idea of whether it is likely to have a greater or lesser effect at that moment. It is important to also explore why the supervisee wants to share trauma details, what they hope to get out of sharing a traumatic story, and whether the supervisor agrees their goal is likely to be achieved. Though many people have the idea that a trauma story reduces in potency the more it is told, it can actually have the opposite effect, and sometimes retelling trauma stories can be detrimental for both supervisee and supervisor.

Instead of telling the whole trauma story, it may help to keep to the titles of a trauma, such as "rape" or "repeated violence from brother." Such limits can often avoid the risk of both the teller and the listener becoming overwhelmed and reduce the risk of vicarious trauma or retraumatization.

EXERCISE Pros and Cons of Telling Trauma Stories

What are the pros and cons of telling details of trauma stories, both for therapy clients and for therapists in their supervision? Details of traumas are not always necessary for healing or understanding, though of course, in some circumstances they are. Listing your opinions on this may help you to discern when this is and is not useful and be able to clearly set that boundary when you feel it is appropriate.

1. List in the space below any pros and cons you can think of for telling trauma stories, maybe listing the specific circumstances that may affect your decision.
   If you are looking for additional ideas around this, you might consider reading *Revolutionizing Trauma Treatment* (Rothschild, 2021).

Pros to telling trauma stories	Cons to telling trauma stories

2. List any boundaries that you wish to put in place for recounting trauma stories as a therapist or supervisor to align with the beliefs you have identified above. *For example, agree with supervisees that they must initially only use titles of trauma stories and the question they want to ask. Then we can decide together whether it is useful or not to hear more details about the trauma story.*
   For example, agree with clients in initial consultations to solely use titles of any trauma stories rather than going into long descriptions that could be retraumatizing for them and cause vicarious trauma for me.

_____

_____

_____

_____

_____

_____

Exercises for Preventing Vicarious Trauma

EXERCISE Current Resources to Avoid Overidentification

We will be exploring a range of strategies to prevent and recover from vicarious trauma in later chapters; however, it may be useful to be aware of the ones you already have.

1. What resources and tools do you currently use to avoid overidentifying with clients? List them in the space below.

   For example, you may already use mindfulness to help you stay present, rather than getting caught up in a story being told. Or you may interrupt your own self-talk, such as "what if that were me," reminding yourself that the story you are listening to is not about you.

   _____

   _____

   _____

   _____

   _____

   _____

   _____

   _____

   _____

   _____

EXERCISE Client Inventory

Taking stock of your caseload can help you to plan appropriate strategies before, during, and after sessions. It can also assist in scheduling so that you have adequate time to recoup between clients who have trauma histories.

1. Look through your current caseload, noting down the titles of clients' trauma histories and their presenting issues.
2. Make a calendar of the days and times you see the clients and consider if their appointment times might be changed to better balance your caseload, such as not seeing clients who are all experiencing similar traumas on the same day, or allowing enough time between sessions to regulate your own autonomic nervous system (ANS), use the bathroom, or have something to eat or drink.

EXERCISE Identifying Symptoms Similar to Your Clients'

1. Check in regularly whether you are experiencing any of the following symptoms, or others, which do not have origin in your own history:
   ☐ Avoiding certain places or people
   ☐ Feeling anxious in ways you do not usually
   ☐ Nightmares or dreams with content of client traumas or issues
   ☐ Emotions such as grief, rage, or sadness that are not connected to your life
   ☐ Risky behavior or self-harm similar to a client's
   ☐ Difficulty sleeping
   ☐ Anxiety attacks
   ☐ Difficulties concentrating or focusing
2. Mark in your diary, or write in the space below, the symptoms you experience and when you experience them.
3. Cross-reference what you have noticed with your client schedule to identify whether these symptoms correspond with a particular client, session, venue, colleague, or other factor.

	Monday	Tuesday	Wednesday	Thursday	Friday	Saturday	Sunday
Morning							
Lunchtime							
Afternoon							
Evening							

Burnout

Definition: Physical and emotional exhaustion caused by stress.

Mo is a lone parent of three children and works as a social worker. Due to financial limitations, they cannot afford childcare during school holidays, and they have no other family, so they use their vacation time to look after the children. Though Mo greatly enjoys this time spent with their children, they have very little time for rest during these breaks. At work, there have been numerous resignations and colleagues on sick leave due to the stressful working conditions. Mo sympathizes with their colleagues; however, management does not replace them, and so the added workload falls to Mo. Because their caseload of vulnerable children is already very high, they take paperwork home to complete when their own children are in bed. Mo often lies awake for much of the night worrying about the work they have not been able to complete, and about the impact that will have on the vulnerable children's lives. It feels like a never-ending cycle of not completing things and not doing tasks as well as they think they should. They feel exhausted but cannot sleep.

Mo increasingly ignores messages and cancels dates with friends, as they feel too exhausted to do anything other than go to work and look after their children. Despite previously loving to cook, they are increasingly using ready-made meals as they don't feel they have the energy to stand in the kitchen or the focus to try new recipes. Initially they noticed that they were short-tempered with colleagues and then later felt they did not have the energy for that.

Eventually, after dropping the children at school, Mo felt they hadn't the energy to walk to the subway to go to work. Instead, they went home and back to bed, calling in sick at work.

Burnout is not restricted to helping professionals. The physical and emotional fatigue described by those who have experienced it can happen to anyone who is overloaded with stress. For those who experience societal oppression, or during times of community and world crisis, such as war, violence, natural disasters, ecological crisis, or pandemics, the risk is heightened.

Recovery from burnout is possible with rest, yet prevention is obviously better than cure. Though Mo's situation means that time for rest and recuperation is incredibly limited, there are strategies that we shall explore in later chapters that can help. It may come as no surprise that the first step, however, is developing awareness of the signs of burnout.

It is important to make clear that many organizational and societal structures can contribute to burnout in ways that you may have limited control over, and that this workbook may not be able to address. When Vanessa started working as a teacher at a new school, she got a postcard from the principal that pictured a teacher at home surrounded by student papers that needed to be graded, with the slogan "work–home balance." It was not meant as the joke it should have been. The message was that the teachers were expected to work all day at school and then grade papers in the evenings at home. Likewise, Mo's social work organization was put in the difficult situation of balancing a high volume of vulnerable and critical caseloads with a decreasing work-force and limited budget. Yet the result for Mo and their coworkers included being overloaded with work, few rewards, little recognition, and a lack of any structure of organizational support.

Maslach and Leiter (1997) found that burnout can begin at the organizational level: "burnout is not a problem of the people themselves but of the social environment in which people work" (p. 18). However, in this workbook, we do not intend to lay blame. Rather our hope is to support you in developing awareness and utilizing helpful strategies where possible. Though there will be factors beyond your immediate control, gaining a sense of control over what you can, may be beneficial.

Exercises for Easing and Preventing Burnout

Having a checklist of potential signs of burnout will help you to develop awareness so that you can intervene before potential burnout becomes an overwhelming problem.

EXERCISE Signs of Burnout Checklist

1. Regularly review the Signs of Burnout Checklist below. You may choose to put these in your journal or in the inside cover of your notes at work.
2. Identify whether you experience none, some, many, or all of the items on the checklist.
3. Over time, monitor whether the number of items on the checklist that you experience increases or decreases.

☐ Feeling tired or drained most of the time

☐ Feeling helpless, trapped, and/or defeated

☐ Feeling out of control or having difficulty making decisions

☐ Feeling that work is chaotic or monotonous

☐ Feeling detached or alone in the world

☐ Becoming more cynical and critical

☐ Self-doubt

☐ Lacking motivation to do previously enjoyable activities

☐ Procrastinating and taking longer to get things done

☐ Feeling overwhelmed

☐ Loss of routine

☐ Loss of enjoyment of activities previously enjoyed

EXERCISE Burnout Contributing Factors Checklist

1. Regularly review the Burnout Contributing Factors Checklist below. You may choose to put these in your journal or in the inside cover of your notes at work.

2. Identify whether you are at risk from none, some, many, or all of the items on the checklist.

3. Over time, monitor whether the number of items on the checklist that relate to you increases or decreases.

☐ Working long hours

☐ A heavy caseload

☐ Difficulties maintaining balance between work and life

☐ Working in a helping profession

☐ Having little control over your work or workload

☐ Having dependents (children or vulnerable adults) outside of work

☐ Commuting a long distance

☐ Multiple jobs

☐ Significant outside-of-work commitments, such as managing clubs/societies, volunteering

☐ Unfilled vacancies at work

☐ Illness

☐ Difficulties sleeping (through stress, noise, etc.)

☐ Working antisocial hours (night shifts, etc.)

☐ Financial pressures

| EXERCISE | Assess Your Current Resources to Prevent Burnout |

You likely already have strategies, people, and hobbies that help to alleviate the feelings associated with burnout. Having awareness of these and when they are effective can be useful. Mo stopped meeting with their friends. Though it would have taken more energy, it is likely that being with friends could offer respite, joy, and a feeling of connectedness that may have helped.

1. What resources and strategies have you used, or do you currently use, that have helped or currently help you to feel the following?

Rested

For example, watching the birds fly outside my window from my desk at regular intervals throughout the day

_____

_____

_____

_____

_____

_____

Enjoying Life

For example, taking a walk on clear evenings to look at the stars

_____

_____

_____

_____

_____

_____

Increased Sense of Strength and Power

For example, riding my bike to work once a week

_____

_____

_____

_____

_____

Connection to Other People and (Other-Than-Human) Nature

For example, arranging lunch dates with friends, and lunch via
videoconferencing with friends that live further away

_____

_____

_____

_____

_____

LACK OF AWARENESS

Developing an awareness of the onset of compassion fatigue, vicarious trauma, or burn-out is essential. Noticing when you are straying from your normal, such as a change in routine, energy levels, sleep, or relationships can signal to you that something is amiss. At this point it is essential to check in with yourself and consider whether you are experiencing any of these three issues.

Throughout the following chapters we share suggestions for self-care strategies and techniques, but, of course, the first step to these is awareness.

Before giving you exercises to improve your awareness, it might be useful to take a look at some of the ways that a lack of awareness could be detrimental to your well-being and the well-being of those you work with.

A lack of awareness while you are working with your clients can cause a variety of problems, including unmanaged countertransference and overempathizing.

Countertransference

Definition: "Reactions to a client that have roots in the practitioner's own past" (Rothschild, 2022).

In his beginning months as a psychotherapist, Toby came to supervision for advice about a client, Thomas, who often got tearful in sessions. When that would happen, Toby would feel a sense of fear and would proceed to try to stop Thomas from crying by telling jokes or changing the subject. Toby was aware enough to know that was not the best helping strategy. Through discussion, Toby and his supervisor found that this response was part of Toby's own history. As a child, whenever Toby was sad about his grandfather's death, his father would distract him by talking about something else or by aggressively telling Toby that "boys don't cry." Thus, he had never been allowed to grieve the loss. In supervision Toby learned that, though kinder than his father, in these situations with his client, Toby was distracting Thomas, as his father had distracted him.

With this new awareness, Toby was better able to monitor his response and use strategies to separate his childhood experience from Thomas's tears. The supervisor also advised Toby to have a few sessions with his own counselor to get therapeutic support for the loss of his grandfather that he had never been allowed to grieve.

Everyone carries painful and difficult experiences from the past, and this pain can be reawakened by experiences in the present. Having the experience of living through and overcoming these past challenges can be useful in developing empathy and understanding for clients. However, when you are unaware that your responses to a client are rooted in your own experiences it can result in problems for both you and your client.

When Toby stopped Thomas from crying, he was preventing his client from expressing grief, similarly to how Toby was not allowed to grieve the loss of his grandfather. Though these feelings were difficult for him to tolerate, the problem was not that he felt fear around other men's sadness, it was his lack of awareness of his automatic response. Once he realized that the response was grounded in his own past, Toby felt much more able to separate his own feelings from Thomas's feelings. That, in turn, made it possible for Thomas to be able to experience and express the sadness he was feeling.

Exercises for Avoiding Out-of-Control Countertransference

EXERCISE Countertransference

Here is a quick exercise that will give you more clarity about some aspects of countertransference.

1. Mindfully check in with yourself to establish a baseline of how you are feeling right now.
2. Choose one of your clients to focus on during this exercise.
3. Remember being with that client, and notice and note down the following as you are aware of them right now:

   • Sensations you feel in your body (hot, cold, achy, prickles, etc.)

   _____

   _____

   • Visual or auditory images that arise in your mind (pictures, colors, sounds, songs, etc.)

   _____

   _____

   • Movement or muscular impulses in your body (head turning, sitting back, legs tensing, clenched fists, etc.)

   _____

   _____

   • Changes in autonomic arousal (breathing, heart rate, temperature of hands and feet, etc.)

   _____

   _____

   • What you feel emotionally (angry, irritated, sad, happy, scared, turned on, disgusted, etc.)

   _____

   _____

• Any thoughts that occur to you

_____

_____

4. Next, take a few minutes to consider which of your responses could be mirrors of your client's experience (sensations, images, behaviors, feelings, thoughts). *For example, if you feel depressed as you think about a depressed client, or if your heart beats a little quicker as you think of an anxious client.*

_____

_____

_____

5. Note any responses (sensations, images, behaviors, feelings, thoughts) that might be countertransference. *For example, where, like Toby, you can identify areas that have links to your own history. Maybe thinking of a client crying causes you to notice that you have dissociated or feel anxious because, in your own past, crying would not have been accepted.*

_____

_____

_____

There is no right or wrong answer for this (or any) exercise in this book. Each point, however, is significant: how you feel about your client and what that client elicits in you.

Feel free to try this exercise with additional clients. It might be interesting to see how your responses differ from client to client. You may also wish to share this and any other exercises in this book with your colleagues or supervisees. It may be a good basis for fruitful discussions and perhaps increased mutual support.

EXERCISE Defining the Risks

Now that you have read a little about the terms compassion fatigue, vicarious trauma, burnout, and countertransference, it might be useful to write, in your own words, a brief example of each one. If possible, add a personal experience of each, maybe with a supervisee, colleague, client, or friend. A personal story can help to illustrate the definition and risk.

Compassion Fatigue

Definition: Emotional exhaustion from prioritizing others' well-being over my own.

For example: When I worked through lunch last week and felt resentful and irritable with the next client I saw.

Example:

_____

_____

_____

Vicarious Trauma

Definition: Experiencing a response or symptoms, such as PTSD, nightmares, or a shift in worldview, as though an event of which the therapist has been told, that is not in their own history, has happened to them.

Example:

_____

_____

_____

Burnout

Definition: Physical and emotional exhaustion caused by stress.

Example:

_____

_____

_____

Countertransference

> **Definition:** Reactions to a client that have roots in the practitioner's own past.

Example:

_____

_____

_____

MINDFUL AWARENESS

> **Definition:** Mindfulness is most commonly defined as present moment awareness without judgment.

Yin came into supervision rubbing her neck and upper back. When asked how she was feeling, she described having a session with a client who is experiencing PTSD symptoms and is often and easily triggered. She had been working on stabilization with them and noting the signs of the client's autonomic nervous system activation so that she could interrupt and help the client stabilize.

However, at the end of the session when they both got up to say goodbye, Yin realized she had been sitting in a very awkward position with her upper back against the corner of the wall and her neck bent around it. Though she had been completely attentive to her client, and purposely had not been resonating, she had entirely missed her own postural discomfort.

You have probably heard the word "mindfulness" before. It is commonly used in yoga, meditation, and psychotherapy, and is an ancient practice. It basically means to have awareness, and it is usually intentional.

Mindful awareness, and lack of awareness, can happen at any time. You have likely experienced both at some time today. Last week, Vanessa went to the movies and halfway through the film pulled her hand out of the popcorn tub, which, she was surprised to discover, was empty. She had eaten it all with no real memory of eating any. She hadn't noticed the salt or the texture or the smell, or even the feeling of fullness in her belly, but she had eaten it all. Meanwhile, she could give a deeply descriptive account of the plot and characters she had watched on the screen. This is a good example of being mindful of the movie while being the opposite, on autopilot, eating the popcorn.

Like Yin, many helping professionals can be great at being mindfully aware of their clients while losing mindful awareness of themselves. This can mean missing physical or emotional discomfort (as described with Yin), overempathizing, or unmanaged countertransference. Over the long-term, such inattention could lead to missing awareness of changes that could indicate burnout, vicarious trauma, or compassion fatigue.

Developing mindful awareness can be useful for helping professionals in many ways, including:

- Mindfulness practices can provide respite, such as in the Choosing Targets Best Suited to You exercise described below.
- Mindful awareness can better enable you to notice your response to your clients and your workload so that you can respond appropriately.
- Mindful awareness can help you choose appropriate self-care strategies and individualize them to best suit your needs.

The following exercises explore mindfulness in these three ways and may assist you in getting started with using mindful awareness to support your self-care. In Chapter 4 we explore the uses and benefits of mindfulness further in Strengthening Your Internal Observer and Developing Dual Awareness.

Exercises to Develop Mindful Awareness

EXERCISE Choosing Targets Best Suited to You

Mindfulness practices can involve a focus on either internal or external phenomena. The object you choose to focus on should be based on what is best suited to you. For example, for some people, being mindful of their breathing can activate feelings of anxiety; for others it can be calming. For some people, using their sense of smell most powerfully holds their awareness, while for others their sense of sight best keeps their focus.

We encourage you to experiment with different senses to find out which is most potent for you; these include senses that take information from the external environment, including sight, hearing, smell, touch, and taste (exteroceptors), the sense of knowing where your body is in space (proprioception), the sense of your internal body sensations (interoceptors), and the sense of balance (vestibular).

We have compiled a list of suggestions for each of the senses for you to experiment with, but we encourage you to adapt these for yourself or to think of other possibilities that would be most suitable for you. The idea is to work out which of these senses is most potent in holding your attention. However, it is also useful if, in addition to holding your focus, it is pleasant. For example, if a scent held your focus because it reminded you of a difficult experience, it might be a useful target, but it could provoke discomfort. It would be preferable to change the difficult scent so that it was one that elicited a neutral or positive feeling. In the exercise for scent described below, Vanessa chose lavender because it reminds her of enjoyable days cycling in France; however, for Babette lavender is reminiscent of a launderette she used in her 20s that was much too hot and busy. So lavender would be a good choice for Vanessa, but not for Babette.

Target sense	Activity	Potency of holding your awareness/focus: 1 (not able to focus at all); 10 (easy to hold focus)
Sight	1. Look around the room where you are and notice an object that draws your attention. 2. Focus on that object. 3. Notice its color(s) and shape(s). 4. Trace its edges with your eyes. 5. Notice where light falls upon it and which parts are in shadow.	1 2 3 4 5 6 7 8 9 10
Sound	1. Notice the loudest sound you can hear right now. 2. Notice when it stops or changes. 3. What is the new loudest sound? 4. What is the softest sound? 5. Notice if the sound changes. 6. Continue to notice the loudest and softest sounds alternately, when they change and what replaces them.	1 2 3 4 5 6 7 8 9 10

Target sense	Activity	Potency of holding your awareness/focus: 1 (not able to focus at all); 10 (easy to hold focus)
Taste	1. Choose a small piece of food with a strong flavor that you find pleasant. Maybe a mint leaf, or piece of orange. 2. Put the piece of food into your mouth and notice the taste. It may be subtle at first. 3. Move it around in your mouth, noticing the taste. 4. Bite, chew, and suck the piece of food. The taste may become stronger as you do this. Focus on the taste. 5. Continue until you are ready to swallow it.	1 2 3 4 5 6 7 8 9 10
Touch	1. Notice the objects around you and choose one that you feel drawn to touch. Maybe a plant, a figurine, a pen. 2. Run your fingers gently over the object, noticing the textures. 3. Is it hard? Soft? Prickly? Smooth? Rough? Bumpy? Furry? 4. Trace the outside edge of the object, noticing any changes in texture.	1 2 3 4 5 6 7 8 9 10
Smell	1. Chose a scent that you like. It may be one that is connected with a pleasant memory. You might use aromatherapy oils, a piece of fruit such as an orange, or an aromatic plant such as lavender, mint, or rosemary. 2. Take 5 easy breaths, smelling the scent on the inhalation.	1 2 3 4 5 6 7 8 9 10

Target sense	Activity	Potency of holding your awareness/focus: 1 (not able to focus at all); 10 (easy to hold focus)
Proprioception 1	This exercise is a little like the game Pin the Tail on the Donkey that you might have played as a child. 1. Choose a spot on a wall and sit or stand an arm length away from it. 2. With your eyes open, touch the spot on the wall, first with one hand, then the other. 3. Next, close your eyes and touch the spot with one hand. Open your eyes to see if your finger is in the correct place. 4. Repeat with the other hand. 5. You could also try throwing a beanbag or ball at a spot on the floor.	1 2 3 4 5 6 7 8 9 10
Proprioception 2	1. Move your awareness through your body to notice internal sensations. These might include a sense of warm, cold, tight, soft, pain, pain-free, fast, slow. 2. Start with your feet and work your way slowly through your whole body to the top of your head. 3. Alternatively, you could choose one body part, such as your belly.	1 2 3 4 5 6 7 8 9 10
Vestibular	1. Choose an object to balance, such as a pen or building block. 2. Balance the object on your hand, two fingers, or one finger, depending on which offers enough challenge to keep you focused but is achievable. 3. Increase the level of challenge to keep your focus. For example, move your finger around, or balance something else on top of the first object.	1 2 3 4 5 6 7 8 9 10

EXERCISE Now I Am Aware

Fritz Perls was the founder of Gestalt therapy and was experienced in Zen philosophy and mindfulness. Thus, "Now I am aware" is a phrase often used in Gestalt exercises. Being mindful is very much about being aware of what is happening in the present moment, which is constantly changing. If I take just a moment as I am typing this now, there is so much change.

Now I am aware that my fingers are moving.

Now I am aware of the feel of the keyboard under one finger and now another.

Now I am aware of a dog barking.

Now I am aware the barking has stopped.

Now I am aware that someone is whistling.

Now I am aware that I feel hungry.

And so on . . .

1. Jot down in the space below what you are aware of in the next 20 to 30 seconds or so, noticing the external environment using your exteroceptors, and noticing any internal or body sensations, such as feeling tension, using your interoceptors.

    Now I am aware _____

    Now I am aware _____

    Now I am aware _____

    Now I am aware _____

    Now I am aware _____

    Now I am aware _____

    Now I am aware _____

    Now I am aware _____

    Now I am aware _____

    Now I am aware _____

    Now I am aware _____

    Now I am aware _____

    Now I am aware _____

    Now I am aware _____

2. Babette and Vanessa also enjoy playing Now I Am Aware as a game, which you could try with your colleagues, partner, children, and clients. It is a good way to help each other stay present and aware.

3. Take turns, with each saying what you are aware of. It can be interesting and fun to find out what the other has noticed in your shared environment that you might not have and how your internal experiences differ.

EXERCISE Mindful Gauge

In *8 Keys to Safe Trauma Recovery* (Rothschild, 2010) and the *8 Keys to Safe Trauma Recovery Workbook* (Rothschild & Bear, 2023), the mindful gauge is introduced as a method of self-awareness. This can be a good tool for helping professionals as well as people who have and have not experienced trauma.

A mindful gauge can help you to identify your reaction to something, particularly when that is difficult to recognize. It can be a body sensation, thought, emotion, mental image, or other identifiable response to a stimulus.

The mindful gauge is especially useful for decision-making. For example, Vanessa was not sure whether to add another client to her caseload. She knew that body sensations are usually a good indicator for her, so she chose that for her mindful gauge. First, she did a quick body scan to notice her current baseline body sensations. Next, she added the new client to her electronic calendar and took a look at that week as a whole. She noticed some tension in her belly at first, but then it relaxed. Next, she deleted the client and checked again. This time her belly relaxed but then tensed a little. The changes in her sensations helped her to realize she was ambivalent. Exploring further, she realized that adding the new client would increase her load and crowd her week a bit, but it would also give her added financial stability and a more diverse caseload. She felt that the benefit would outweigh the challenge and decided to see the new client.

Developing a mindful gauge can help with making a variety of personal as well as professional decisions; for example, when to rest, what to eat, whether to take on a new client, identifying if you need to implement a self-care strategy with a specific client, or recognizing your own current needs. Below are exercises that will help you identify your strongest mindful gauge or gauges.

1. Decide on two things to choose from. While you are initially exploring your mindful gauge, it is useful to try choices that are benign, such as choosing to read the

novel or the biography, if you would prefer to wear the striped top or the plain top, or whether to eat a banana or a pear. Write the options in the boxes below.

	Option 1			Option 2	
Body sensations	Tight chest	Soft belly	Lengthened spine	Faster heartbeat	Fidgety
	Stiffness	Numbness	Soft eyes	Sighing	Holding breath
	Soft muscles	Cold feet	Steady heartbeat	Pain/aching	Sweaty
Thoughts, poems, sayings, analogies, songs	I cannot do it	I love the …	I hate it	This reminds me of …	I wish it were …
	I do not like …	I am glad it is …	I prefer …	I do not understand …	I need to …
	Later I will …				
Emotions	Angry	Cheerful	Cranky	Frustrated	Excited
	Energized	Peaceful	Uncomfortable	Sleepy	Sad
	Disgusted	Withdrawn	Revolted	Anxious	Nervous
	Afraid	Cozy	Confused	Satisfied	
Mind's images: memories of smells, tastes, sounds, sights, inner impulses	Option 1 *Draw or describe **any** image(s) that come to mind when you focus your attention on this option.*			Option 2 *Draw or describe **any** image(s) that come to mind when you focus your attention on this option.*	
Any other noticeable reactions					

2. Next, consider each option individually. For example, if it is a choice between eating a pear and a banana, take some time to look at the pear, feel its texture, maybe smell it.

3. Notice any change in the gauge you are using. For example, if your focus was body sensation, maybe you notice your mouth watering. We suggest that you focus on one of the responses at a time. For example, just notice your body sensations, or just your emotions. Use the same gauge for both options.

4. Do the same process for the other option.

5. Based on your responses, make your choice.

6. Test out whether it was the correct choice. If you chose banana based on the positive response, does it still feel like it was the correct choice once you are eating it?

7. Repeat this with different options and experimenting with the different gauges (body sensation, thought, emotion, mental image) to find which gauge or gauges works best for you. It is likely that one or two gauges will offer more significant responses than the others.

We suggest you use your mindful gauge throughout this workbook and, where possible, at least one time each day. Once you feel confident in your mindful gauge, it will often function automatically.

EXERCISE   Awareness of Your Current Resources

It can be easy to lose track of the things that cultivate a sense of calm, joy, wonder, and strength. Life happens, our routines change, and nourishing people and activities get lost in the process. Helping professionals tend to be fantastic at encouraging the identification and use of resources for their clients, but not so good at doing it for themselves.

It can be useful to do an inventory of your own resources, as well as how they tend to make you feel. Keep this list handy so that you can choose any appropriate resources that will most likely offer what you need when you need it.

Resources could be activities, people, animal companions, places, coping strategies, or whatever is useful to your well-being. Add your current resources to the table below. If it makes more sense to you to have a different layout, create your own table.

	Resources	What feelings does this resource cultivate for you?
Functional resources I have	For example: locks on doors and windows, regularly serviced car, cell phone, personal alarm, financial stability	For example: calm, confidence, strength, connection, wonder, joy, safety, stability
Physical resources I have	For example: exercise class, dancing, gardening, walking, singing, painting, ceramics	For example: calm, confidence, strength, connection, wonder, joy, safety, stability
Interpersonal resources I have	For example: knowing my neighbors, part of community or activity group, humans and animals that have supported or do support me	For example: calm, confidence, strength, connection, wonder, joy, safety, stability
Psychological resources I have	For example: mindfulness, therapy sessions, self-help information	For example: calm, confidence, strength, connection, wonder, joy, safety, stability
Spiritual resources I have	For example: yoga, meditation, sitting in nature, going to a place of worship, watching birds, listening to music, gardening	For example: calm, confidence, strength, connection, wonder, joy, safety, stability

EXERCISE Alternative Resources

Valentino noticed that he had started to lose confidence and motivation. He had experienced a bout of flu which had shifted his usual routine, and since returning to work he had not gotten back to normal. His caseload at work had suddenly increased on his return and he was feeling exhausted. Prior to being ill, he went on 30-minute jogs in the park each day, which helped him to feel strong in his body. After a jog, he sat on a bench watching passers-by and noticing nature around him, which brought him a sense of calm.

He considered that the lack of confidence, motivation, and energy might be connected with not doing these activities but did not feel he had the energy to jog for 30 minutes. He contemplated what other activities brought a feeling of strength and decided to start with 5-minute walks through the park, with the bench sitting afterwards. Though there was a pang of disappointment that he was unable to jog yet, walking and the bench time was enough to bring back some of the feelings of strength and energy and gradually build them up again.

Noticing the feeling you want to cultivate can be useful in choosing the activity or person you spend time with. Like Valentino, you might notice that you miss running, which helped you to feel strong, but do not have time or energy for it. Looking down your list for shorter and less challenging options may help with finding a compromise.

Consider the resources you have recorded above and the activities that you noted in the exercise Finding Nourishment earlier in this chapter, and add resources and potential alternatives that can help to cultivate these feelings for you. If these feelings are not ones that you would prioritize for your well-being, then cross out our suggestions and replace with your own.

Calm	Wonder	Strength	Joy	Connection

EXERCISE · Keeping a Mindful Eye on Yourself

Using mindful awareness during therapy sessions with your clients can help you to notice your current state. It might be that, like Yin, your focus on your client takes priority, and your own unease is missed. Taking time to notice yourself can help you to stay calm, grounded, and present during sessions. It might be that you do this without your client knowing. Alternatively, it could become something you include in your sessions to do at the same time as your client. After all, being calm, grounded, and present is useful to both of you.

1. Set a soft alarm on your phone or invest in a bracelet that vibrates according to a timer, or a meditation type of alarm clock or phone app (they chime at programmed intervals) to make a sound or vibration at certain intervals during the session, maybe every 10 minutes.

   This could be something that only you are aware of, such as a gentle vibrating alarm, or it can be something you can discuss with your clients and introduce for both of you.

2. When the alarm chimes, take two or three breaths, and check in with how you are feeling. You might choose to use the mindful gauge we described earlier in this chapter, choosing one of the gauges to focus on, or signs from your autonomic nervous system. If it would be useful to you, Babette's Autonomic Nervous System Precision Regulation chart (Rothschild, 2021) can be found in the revised edition of the original *Help for the Helper* that this workbook accompanies (Rothschild, 2022).

3. Notice whether you can do or change something to feel more calm, comfortable, and present. For example, Yin might have changed the way she was sitting.

   Right now, I notice (use the blank space to add any sensations you notice that aren't listed):

Body Sensations	Tight chest	Soft belly	Lengthened spine	Faster heartbeat	Fidgety
	Stiffness	Numbness	Soft eyes	Sighing	Holding breath
	Soft muscles	Cold feet	Steady heartbeat	Pain/aching	Sweaty

Thoughts, poems, sayings, analogies, songs	I cannot . . .	I love the . . .	I hate . . .	This reminds me of . . .	I wish it were . . .
	I do not like . . .	I am glad it is . . .	I prefer . . .	I do not understand . . .	I need to . . .
	Later I will . . .				
Emotions	Angry	Cheerful	Cranky	Frustrated	Excited
	Energized	Peaceful	Uncomfortable	Sleepy	Sad
	Disgusted	Withdrawn	Revolted	Anxious	Nervous
	Afraid	Cozy	Confused	Satisfied	
Mind's images: memories of smells, tastes, sounds, sights, inner impulses	Draw or describe any image(s) in your mind right now.				
Any other noticeable reactions					

Recognizing your risk factors and engaging your mindful awareness will lay a firm foundation for making use of the theory and tools to come in the following chapters.

CHAPTER 2

Managing the Ties That Bind

EMPATHY

This chapter explores the mechanisms of empathy, the effect it has on you as a helping professional, and how to modulate your own level of empathy. While the benefits of empathy are widely understood, it is less well known that empathy can also take a heavy emotional toll. Resources to manage empathy, as well as its accompanying risks of emotional contagion and vicarious trauma, are essential for both your well-being and longevity in your chosen profession.

Defining Empathy

Vanessa remembers a school lesson when she was eight years old. The teacher explained that sympathy was to feel sad or bad for someone who is having a challenging time, while empathy is like stepping into their shoes and feeling everything that they are feeling. Vanessa remembers trying to imagine leaving her body and melding into someone else's. It was a tricky feat at that age.

Among academics, there are many disagreements about what empathy is and how it is defined. The definition that we will use is similar to that of Vanessa's teacher, though it is actually taken from *Merriam-Webster*'s dictionary (2024):

> The action of understanding, being aware of, being sensitive to, and vicariously experiencing the feelings, thoughts, and experience of another of either the past or present without having the feelings, thoughts, and experience fully communicated in an objectively explicit manner.

This definition, itself, suggests the potential hazards, particularly for professionals who are regularly helping individuals with overwhelmed and dysregulated nervous systems.

Empathy Is a Double-Edged Sword

Empathy is brilliant in allowing people to understand each other better, to see from another's perspective, and to have insight into their life. Of course, this is incredibly useful for helping professionals in particular, in some cases enabling better assistance to those they work with.

However, empathy can be a double-edged sword. The definition from *Merriam-Webster*'s dictionary above shows the potential for danger: "*vicariously* experiencing the feelings, thoughts, and experience of another." Stepping into the shoes of another person who is overwhelmed, dysregulated, traumatized, anxious, feeling helpless or depressed risks a vicarious experience of those very same feelings.

A single instance of this might be unpleasant, but the potential for a more harmful impact from ongoing, regular, and repeated instances is an ever-present risk for helping professionals. Measuring your degree of empathy as if it is on a dial will help you to modulate it to your advantage. The empathy dial as a useful tool will be discussed later in this chapter in the section "Your Personal Empathy Dial." Nevertheless, as a starting point, consider that taking conscious control of your personal empathy dial, how deeply you empathize, is essential. Not only will that put you in charge, but it will also require that you stay alert to how much you are empathizing. Mindful self-awareness is always protective when working in demanding situations.

Having your empathy dial turned up on high can, of course, sometimes be very pleasant.

> *Jamila went out of her office for lunch. Walking down the street, she passed a park where she saw a group of children and adults singing and dancing, surrounded by flowers and balloons. As Jamila passed, one of the children smiled and waved and danced. Jamila smiled and waved back and found herself copying the dance. Walking on, Jamila felt a deep sense of warmth, joy, and connection, which stayed with her for the rest of the day.*

Compassion Versus Empathy

The *Merriam-Webster*'s dictionary (2024) definition of compassion is "sympathetic consciousness of others' distress together with a desire to alleviate it." Rather than a vicarious experience of their suffering, as with empathy, compassion can be a way to offer others support without sharing in their suffering. For an analogy, think about empathy as like jumping into and getting caught up in a whirlpool with your client, whereas compassion is more like standing on the side, witnessing, and being concerned about their difficulty while at the same time being in a better position to help them get out. Empathy is feeling *with* someone, while compassion is caring *about* someone.

With close friends and family, both empathy and compassion can be important ways to connect. With babies and infants, empathy is an important factor in early bonding with their primary caregiver. However, as helping professionals, it can be more beneficial to be able to be stable and present enough to support and help clients, to be able to think clearly when they cannot. They need you to be standing steady on the edge of the whirlpool rather than floundering inside it with them.

For many other professions too, compassion rather than empathy is paramount. If a surgeon or veterinarian were to empathize with a patient, it would be impossible for them to carry out procedures, particularly painful ones, at the same time as feeling what their patient might feel. Instead, they require a great deal of compassion to undertake such long training and working hours, often working in life-and-death conditions.

EXERCISE   Compassion or Empathy

1. Identify and circle which of the following statements would be a compassionate response and which would be empathetic.
2. Add additional examples of your own for each of the blank boxes in the table.

1. *I can feel how hard that is.*	Compassion / Empathy
2. *I understand how hard that is for you.*	Compassion / Empathy
3. *Helper notices client has tears in their eyes.*	Compassion / Empathy
4. *Helper has tears in their eyes, as well as the client.*	Compassion / Empathy
5. *I feel afraid listening to your story.*	Compassion / Empathy
6. *I understand that experiencing that would have been scary, and wish to help you manage your ongoing PTSD symptoms.*	Compassion / Empathy

7. *The level of stress you describe causes my heart rate to increase and palms to sweat.*	Compassion / Empathy
8. *I recognize that you are stressed and have some suggestions on how to manage it.*	Compassion / Empathy
	Compassion
	Empathy

(Answers: 1, empathy; 2, compassion; 3, compassion; 4, empathy; 5, empathy; 6, compassion; 7, empathy; 8, compassion)

Somatic Empathy

It is common for people to have experiences similar to Jamila's. It is a very human phenomenon. Many therapists, including ourselves, have spent time with friends or with clients and felt like we have "caught" their emotions. However, with an understanding of how empathy works, and with practice, you will be able to choose whether you catch, or are infected by, someone else's emotions or not. And then if you are, you will have more knowledge of what to do about it.

In the rest of this chapter, we shall explore how the link between body, mind, and emotions creates empathy, and how you can feel more in control of the degree of empathy you allow. The exercises below are designed to help you to regulate your empathy dial to maximize the beneficial effects of empathy and minimize the adverse and risky effects.

EMOTIONS AND FEELINGS: THE BODY AND THE MIND

To understand somatic empathy, it is useful to first understand the link between mind and body, particularly in relation to emotions and feeling. In Chapter 3 we shall discuss the sensory nervous system further, yet it may be useful to have some awareness of the basics.

Somatic Markers

A *somatic marker* is simply a way in which your body remembers your past. For example, Jamila gets a nice feeling in her stomach when she smells cinnamon, which is a somatic marker for memories of baking with her aunt when she was young.

Above, Vanessa's teacher's description of empathy as stepping into the body of another person is at least partially accurate. Empathy seems to be rooted in the resonance or mirroring of a somatic experience, and consequently in feeling the emotions of another. Research points to the significance of this relationship of body-to-body empathy.

Antonio Damasio (1994, 1999) theorizes that each emotion can be directly linked to a somatic experience, including body sensations, movement, and muscular engagement. He also states that each emotion is connected with autonomic nervous system (ANS) responses that may not be observable by another person, such as increased heart rate, or the temperature of hands and feet.

It can be useful for you to have awareness of this, particularly when it is difficult to name an emotion. This is also the first step in understanding how you might "catch" another's feelings, as will be discussed later in this chapter.

The following exercise offers a demonstration of Damasio's theory.

EXERCISE   Notice Your Somatic Markers for Feeling Happy

1. Recall a recent or past memory of being happy.
2. Focus on that memory, noticing what you remember from your five senses (sight, hearing, touch, taste, smell). Note it in the spaces provided below.
   For example, Toni's memory is being by a lake they visited with their best friend during the first summer of college.

Place: _____

For example, a lake.

Memories of what you saw: _____

_____

For example, tall green trees, clear water, mountains in the distance, best friend laughing and splashing in the water.

Memories of what you heard: _____

_____

For example, birds singing, the sound of the breeze in the leaves, friend's laughter.

Memories of anything you touched or felt on your skin: _____

_____

For example, warm breeze on face, soft shirt against skin.

Memories of anything you tasted: _____

_____

For example, taste of lemon drops.

Memories of any aromas or odors: _____

_____

For example, lemon, pine.

3. As you activate your sensory memory of that event, notice the response in your body right now and note it below in the relevant category. These are your somatic markers for that event. You may wish to notice just one or two of these categories at a time.
   For example, as Toni remembered being at the lake, they noticed their shoulders and jaw soften, they felt warmth in their chest and stomach, noticed a gentle smile, and took a deep sighing breath.

   Body sensations _____

   Breath _____

   Muscle _____

   Heart rate _____

Hands and feet temperature _____

Movement _____

Posture _____

Facial expression _____

EXERCISE Notice Your Somatic Markers for
Feeling More Difficult Emotions

Next, experiment with noticing your somatic responses with different emotions. We recommend that you *lightly* explore a difficult feeling. Choose a memory that is not at all traumatic, but rather a very minor stress, such as having a mildly uncomfortable conversation or conflict.

1. Bring to mind a memory of a minor stress that took place in the past 24 hours when you felt frustrated or irritated.

2. As with the previous exercise, note the memory of your five senses from that experience.

   Place: _____
   For example, a store.

   See: _____
   For example, a long line of people, one cashier open, many tills closed.

   Hear: _____
   For example, cars outside, people in the line sighing and huffing.

   Feel: _____
   For example, uncomfortable tight shoes, the breath of the person waiting behind you in the line.

   Taste: _____
   For example, mint from the gum you were chewing.

   Smell: _____
   For example, perspiration.

3. As you remember that event, use your sensory awareness to notice your current somatic markers for that event in your body and write them below in the relevant category. You may wish to notice just one or two body responses at a time.

4. If you wish to experiment with other emotions, such as fear or sadness, we recommend you use memories that are not traumatic. Follow the same guidelines as above.

5. Share your findings with friends and colleagues, and notice whether their somatic responses are similar to yours. Notice any differences.

Caveat: The idea here is to experience the connection between sensory memory and current body responses, somatic markers; it is not intended for you to become uncomfortable or triggered!

For example, Toni remembered standing in line in the store, on a very hot day when they were in a rush. Although they made it to their next meeting in time after all, when they remember the feeling of irritation that so many checkout lanes were closed, they still feel hot and sweaty, have a dry mouth, their respiration and heart rate increase, and their muscles feel tight.

Frustrated or Irritated

Body sensations _____

Breath _____

Muscle _____

Heart rate _____

Hands and feet temperature _____

Movement _____

Posture _____

Facial expression _____

Afraid

For example, at the fairground, Jamila's friends all wanted to go on the roller coaster. Though she knew it would be safe, she felt a pang of fear. She ended up enjoying the thrilling experience, but when she remembered looking up at the roller coaster, she could still feel tightness in her belly and muscles, her heart rate increased, and her hands and feet felt cold.

Body sensations _____

Breath _____

Muscle _____

Heart rate _____

Hands and feet temperature _____

Movement _____

Posture _____

Facial expression _____

Sad

For example, when Jamila recalls saying goodbye to her friend who moved to a different state a month ago, she notices tears in her eyes, her spine rounds, the sides of her mouth turn down, her body feels sluggish and slow, her breathing slows down, and she takes some sighing exhales.

Body sensations _____

Breath _____

Muscle _____

Heart rate _____

Hands and feet temperature _____

Movement _____

Posture _____

Facial expression _____

Emotion and Feeling

In English, the words "emotion" and "feeling" are often used interchangeably to refer to affects of all sorts; however, Damasio (1994, 1999) sees a distinction. He identifies emotion as the somatic changes that occur in response to an associated affect. Such changes may include sensations, shifts in the ANS, and contraction or relaxation in muscles that may or may not result in movement. When those changes in the body become conscious in the mind, that is what Damasio defines as a feeling.

For example, the tension in your jaw and shoulders might express anger but not be experienced as the feeling of anger until you become aware of those sensations and muscle tensions. In essence, Damasio asserts that *a feeling is the awareness of an emotion.*

EXERCISE Notice What You Already Know About the Links Between Body, Emotion, and Feelings

For each of the feelings listed, write the various somatic and autonomic responses you would expect to observe in another or feel in yourself.

Sadness

	What you expect to observe
Facial expression	
Posture	
Breathing rate (quick, shallow, steady, etc.)	
Heart rate	
Temperature of hands and feet	
Ability to be in contact with others: Possible/ unlikely/ withdrawn/ limited	

Happiness

	What you expect to observe
Facial expression	
Posture	
Breathing rate (quick, shallow, steady, etc.)	
Heart rate	
Temperature of hands and feet	
Ability to be in contact with others: Possible/ unlikely/ withdrawn/ limited	

Anger

	What you expect to observe
Facial expression	
Posture	
Breathing rate (quick, shallow, steady, etc.)	
Heart rate	
Temperature of hands and feet	
Ability to be in contact with others: Possible/ unlikely/ withdrawn/ limited	

Fear

	What you expect to observe
Facial expression	
Posture	
Breathing rate (quick, shallow, steady, etc.)	
Heart rate	
Temperature of hands and feet	
Ability to be in contact with others: Possible/ unlikely/ withdrawn/ limited	

EXERCISE Observing the Somatic Responses of Others

Actors tend to be exceptionally good at portraying somatic responses and can offer an easy way to carefully observe another without it feeling intrusive.

Watch a television program and notice whether your expectations from the previous exercise fit with what you observe. Alternatively, you could watch a reality television program to observe people who are not acting.

FACIAL AND POSTURAL FEEDBACK

Dr. Paul Ekman (1972) researched people of diverse cultures, languages, and ethnicities and found that facial expressions were intrinsically linked with emotional states and, further, that these were universal. Prior to development of verbal language, this is how we communicated our feelings, and it is how animals communicate their feelings. The idea that specific human expressions are universally understood means that we can make a good guess about other people's internal experience. You likely have experienced being able to tell when a friend is in a bad mood or a colleague is upset, just by looking at their facial expression.

While doing the previous exercise, Vanessa noticed that when she remembered feeling sad after her greenhouse collapsed and destroyed the seedlings that she had been cultivating for weeks, her spine was rounded, shoulders hunched, and mouth turned down.

Interestingly, the theory of *facial feedback* (Ekman et al., 1983) asserts that just as emotion causes a particular facial expression, a particular facial expression can cause the corresponding emotional response. For example, when Babette turned the corners of her mouth up, she noticed a gentle lift in her spirits. In 1995, Dr. Madan Kataria started Laughter Yoga, working on facial feedback principles to first fake or simulate laughter, which, research has shown, turns into real laughter and results in reduced stress, burnout levels, and blood pressure as well as increased quality of life.

Another interesting example involves research on the effect of smiling. People were instructed to hold a pencil horizontally in their mouths, forcing the sides of their mouth upward into a smile. The research found that doing so increased the feeling of happiness or laughter. Alternatively, when they were instructed to hold a pencil with the tip between their teeth, sadness and other negative emotions increased (Strack et al., 1988).

EXERCISE   Explore Facial Feedback for Yourself

1. For each of the facial expressions in the chart below, consider the emotion being depicted.
2. You could compare your answers with those of a friend or colleague. Notice the similarities and differences.
3. Take a moment to notice your current body sensations, mood, thoughts, and facial expression.
4. One at a time, copy the facial expressions in the chart.
5. Notice whether your body sensations, mood, and thoughts have changed or stayed the same.
6. Next time you are watching television or a movie, choose a character's facial expression to copy. Notice whether your own mood or body sensations change.
7. If you have noticed a negative change in feeling, consciously change your expression to one that has a positive result for you when you've finished the exercise.

	Feeling depicted (happy, sad, angry, bored, surprised, afraid, etc.)	Feeling and body sensation change when copying the facial expression
😟		
😠		
🙂		
😧		
😄		
😮		
🙂		
😐		

While extensive discussion is not within the scope of this book, it may be useful to be aware that research has shown that individuals with autism spectrum disorder (ASD) may not have the same response with facial feedback, some research indicates that autistic people may have unique facial expressions unlike those of people who are not autistic (Yirmiya et al., 1992). Later studies have expanded on this to suggest that autistic people may have a different feedback system specific to these facial expressions (Stel et al., 2008).

Postural Feedback

Postural feedback works similarly. When sad, people tend to drop their shoulders and round or hunch their spine; when happy, their chest tends to be slightly lifted, with an upright spine. As with facial expressions, when posture is changed, emotion often changes to correspond.

EXERCISE Experiment With Postural Feedback

1. Take a moment to notice your current body sensations, mood, thoughts, and posture.
2. Imitate the postures in the following chart one at a time.
3. Spend a minute or so in each posture.

	Feeling (happy, sad, angry, bored, confident, afraid, etc.)	Feeling and body sensation change when copying the posture

4. Notice how you feel. Are your body sensations the same as or different from the start of the exercise?

5. If possible for you, try each one standing up, walking, and sitting down.

6. Next time you are watching a television show or a movie, choose a character's posture to copy. Notice whether your own mood or body sensations change.

7. If you have noticed a negative change in feeling, it is likely useful to consciously change your posture to one that has a positive response for you when you've finished the exercise.

EXERCISE   Postural Resource

Have you ever tried mimicking a Superman or Wonder Woman posture before facing a challenging situation, such as giving a talk or asking for a raise? In some circles this is a popular and common ritual. You might try it for yourself and see if it bolsters your confidence or courage in advance of a situation where that might be useful.

1. Check in with how you are feeling—your emotions and mood.

2. Set a timer for one minute. Stand or sit in a posture similar to a superhero, with your chin, spine, and chest lifted, maybe hands on hips, and if standing, feet hip width apart.

3. When the time is up, check in with your emotions and mood. Consider whether it changed positively. If so, consider when it might be useful to practice this. If you would like to read more about using the Wonder Woman posture, here is one article to try: https://www.harpersbazaar.com/uk/wellness/a36820/how-standing-like-wonder-woman-can-boost-your-confidence/.

MIMICRY AND MIRRORING

Mimicking others is something that occurs from early life. When Vanessa was training in child psychotherapy, a requirement of the training was to observe an infant for two years. She found a young family nearby with a new baby, and the mother agreed that Vanessa could visit regularly to observe her child. During the initial session, Vanessa noticed the mother's foot moving in a particular rhythm. A few seconds later, the baby on her lap also started to wiggle his foot in the same rhythm. Likewise, Vanessa also observed the mother mirroring her baby's facial expressions and body language, smiling, yawning, and so on, along with her child. Kohut (1971) described this early mimicking and mirroring as essential for a baby to develop a sense of self; it can also increase attunement between mother and child (Gallese, 2007).

From early childhood, mirroring others continues, often unconsciously. It enables us to learn tasks, attune to each other, and feel connected.

A colleague of ours consciously used mirroring in job interviews for this reason. She believes that some of her success in getting the jobs she wanted could be attributed to her mirroring the interviewer's expressions and postures. She believes that strategy contributes to a sense of alliance. Though mirroring has these obvious advantages, it also has disadvantages, which we shall explore later in this chapter.

Often, a therapist will have a sense of attunement with a client, or believe they know the client's internal experience. Is that intuition? Perhaps, but at least in part, it is likely that such experiences can be explained by facial and/or postural feedback, Damasio's somatic marker theory, and the theory of mirror neurons.

Mirror neurons are a type of motor neuron. Research on these fascinating neurons has suggested that they fire when one person is observing another person's movements. The result is that the observer can feel the same muscular sensations as the one who is active. You might have noticed this yourself when, for example, you have watched sports. If your arms or legs tense as you see downhill skiing, your breathing quickened during a racing competition, or you felt your arm flinch as the Wimbledon competitor hit a backhand, you have experienced the effect of mirror neurons.

Such mirroring processes may also underlie the way in which psychotherapists are affected by the emotional states of their clients. They might unconsciously synchronize breathing, posture, or facial expressions. Since, as we explored earlier, somatic markers and body movements have direct links to feelings, such unconscious mirroring can result in simultaneous experience of the same emotions.

Unconscious mirroring happens all the time. It is one of the main ways that we are able to learn from and about each other, connect with one another, and stay safe. Humans are social animals. It is in our best interest to connect as part of a group in case of illness, for food gathering, for shelter building, and in case of danger. If one member of our group senses danger, mirror neurons respond by activating the same threat response throughout the group.

EXERCISE Observe Mimicry

Babette went for a coffee in a café this morning. She observed a couple of women chatting together and unconsciously synchronizing their movements as if they were dancers. One crossed a leg over her thigh and soon after the other did too; one smiled and then the other. One leaned in to speak, and the other leaned in toward her. One got a notification of a message on her phone and frowned at the screen; the other frowned and narrowed her eyebrows. Checking in with herself, Babette also noticed her own eyebrows had drawn together, eyes narrowed, and her mouth had formed a frown.

Try this for yourself:

1. In a café, at a family meal, in a park, or some such, observe two people talking together.

2. Notice how they mirror one another. When one changes position, does the other follow suit? Do they reflect each other's facial expressions or breathe in synchrony? What happens for you when you notice that? Do you also mirror the same? Do you make any assumptions about their relationship?

3. Are there any couples not mirroring? What happens for you when you notice that? Do you make any assumptions about their relationship?

EXERCISE Explore Mirroring for Yourself

1. Next time you are in conversation with a friend or family member, notice your body position and theirs. What happens when you change your position? How does it feel if they do or do not mirror you?

_____

_____

_____

_____

2. Next time you are in conversation with someone and feel a sense of connection or attunement, notice how you are mirroring each other: facial expressions, posture, breathing, and so on.

_____

_____

_____

_____

EXERCISE   Explore Mirroring in Nature

Vanessa finds being mirrored by other-than-human nature offers a greater understanding of her experience as well as a sense of being seen and validated. For example, this morning Vanessa was feeling tired and a little sad about some difficult news. On her daily walk she noticed a tree that had been blown over in the wind, with rain dropping heavily onto its drooping leaves. Vanessa felt a sense of her internal experience being mirrored by the tree. That, in turn, increased her awareness of her own feelings. Next, she realized how she would like to help the tree, which helped her to recognize the kind of support that she would like for herself. Vanessa has experienced similar mirroring in nature with both difficult and pleasant emotions.

You might try this yourself:

1. Go outdoors for a walk or look out the window.
2. See if you can find something that reflects your current mood or feelings. What do you notice about it?
3. If you are being mirrored, how do you feel? Is there any message or meaning?
4. Draw what mirrored you or write something from its perspective about how it is feeling and what it needs right now.

In her training programs, Babette sometimes shows a television advertisement where different iterations of facial expressions are shown using everyday objects such as door handles for noses and windows for eyes. It is fun to observe the faces of the training participants mirror the expressions of the inanimate objects as they watch the brief film.

1. The next time you are watching television or a movie, periodically pause to notice the facial expression you have and compare it to that of the person you see on-screen.
2. Find one or more advertisements (in magazines, on billboards, or as you watch television) that utilize inanimate objects to provoke your emotions. The desk lamp in the Pixar logo is just one example.

Mirroring and Empathy

A British illusionist, Derren Brown, uses psychological approaches in his performances. One episode of *Trick or Treat* (aired April 13, 2007) involved two strangers in adjoining rooms able to see each other through a glass partition. Person A was instructed to do whatever they chose, move around, make drinks, and so on. Person B was instructed to copy everything Person A did, including facial expression and body posture. After some time had passed, they faced each other, and Person A was asked to silently remember a heroic event. Person B was then asked to say what he was feeling and imagining at that moment; he described feeling happiness and relief. These descriptions fit the actual experience of Person A, who was remembering when he rescued someone who had fallen onto a train track, saving their life. Mirroring for just a short amount of time facilitated Person B to get a sense of an impactful experience of Person A and allowed them to share similar emotions, without any verbal dialogue.

EXERCISE Mirroring and Empathy

This exercise offers an exploration similar to what the British illusionist facilitated. It will give you an opportunity to experiment with the potency of mirroring for yourself. Similar to that experiment, make sure you use a positive memory, which will elicit positive feelings in the person being mirrored. Absolutely do not use a traumatic one.

1. Partner with a friend or colleague. You can take turns to each try mirroring. Decide who will be Person A, the person being mirrored, and Person B, the person copying Person A.

2. Before you begin, each of you should check in with yourself to notice how you are feeling: mood, sensations, and so on.

3. Next, start with Person A doing some slow, easy-to-follow, simple movements, such as walking back and forth, drinking water, or so on; and Person B carefully copying each movement.

4. After a few minutes of Person B copying Person A, sit or stand facing each other.

5. Person A: Remember a potent memory of being happy, confident, or successful.

6. Person B: Notice any body sensations, mood changes, emotions, and feelings as you continue to face Person A.

7. Person B: Report on what you have experienced and make a guess about what Person A was remembering.

8. Person A: Report on your own experience and briefly share the memory. Repeat all steps with the roles reversed.

CONTROLLING EMPATHY, MIRRORING, AND MIMICRY

Mindful Awareness Check-In

The first step in gaining control of your well-being is to further develop your self-awareness. A therapist's physical, mental, and emotional capacity can change from one day to the next, and from one client to the next, and it is important to notice such changes so you can adjust to meet your needs. For example, if you are feeling exhausted at the end of the day, it may not be a good time for you, or your client, to embark on an energetic or potentially intense intervention. Or if during a break between clients you received bad news, you are likely to have different needs than before the difficult call.

To ensure that you are able to best assess your current needs, you need to be able to pay mindful attention to yourself in the moment. it can be helpful to your continued well-being to check in and notice how you are each day, before, during, and after sessions with clients.

Take note if you already have a practice for this, and make sure it is in your toolbox, along with the next exercise. We encourage you to adjust and individualize this and any exercise to suit yourself; for example, if noticing sensations in your feet is not possible or useful, perhaps notice only your toes, or shift awareness to your hands, and so on.

EXERCISE   Mindful Check-In

1. Wiggle your toes, move your feet around, and notice the texture of what is against the skin of your feet—your socks, the insides of your shoes, or the floor. Feel whatever it is: rough, soft, hard, cold, warm, and so on.

2. Assess your current body position. Are you slouched, upright, or sitting with the natural curvatures of your spine? Are your feet flat on the floor or curled under you? Are you sitting straight or crooked?

3. Notice your facial expression. If you were looking at your face in a mirror, what mood or emotion would you guess you were feeling?

4. Notice your thoughts. Are they racing, sluggish, distracted, chaotic, calm, reasonable?

5. Notice your emotion and mood: happy, sad, angry, afraid, and so on.

6. What is your current energy level right now? Are you feeling energized, tired, somewhere in between, exhausted?

7. Notice body sensations. Are any parts of your body sore, aching, painful, tense, relaxed, comfortable, numb?

8. How is your breathing? Shallow, quick, easy, deep, slow?

This check-in might alert you to something that will support you, or be useful for you to do or not do. For example, if you realize you have a sore shoulder, you may want to gently move it periodically during your day or ask for help with any heavy lifting. If you notice your breathing is fast and shallow and you are feeling anxious, it might be wise and caring to take some time, even if only a few minutes, to do a calming or soothing activity.

EXERCISE Self-Awareness in the Presence of Others

Holding self-awareness in the presence of another person is a vital skill that many therapists lack. It is most usual for professionals to keep their attention on their clients, not on themselves. However, this is a skill that can be developed through practice.

1. Ask a friend or colleague to take part in this exercise with you. If no one is available, look at a photo of someone you have a connection with, or even try it while watching a television show.
2. Sit or stand, wiggle your toes, allow your spine to lengthen.
3. Bring awareness to either your mood, your body sensations, or your thoughts.
4. Ask your partner to walk into your field of view and face you. Notice whether it is possible for you to stay grounded and present, while also being aware of your partner.
5. Ask your partner to walk away, and then back into your field of view to face you again. Once this exercise is over, continue to practice being able to stay in contact with your own experience when another person is present in various situations. We shall further explore this when exploring dual awareness in Chapter 4.
6. Once you gain confidence keeping awareness of yourself in a nonprofessional capacity, take this skill into the therapeutic space and practice holding awareness of yourself at the same time you are aware of your client. In the beginning, it might help to alternate your awareness between yourself and your client. Be patient as it may take a while to develop comfort and confidence in doing this, but if you keep at it, you will likely be able to.

Tip: Mindful Reminder
A reminder to check in with yourself can be helpful, as it can be difficult to remember, particularly if paying attention to yourself is new. Setting an alarm to sound or vibrate every 10 minutes or so can be useful for this. If it is loud enough for your client to hear, you could contract with them to use the alert as a reminder for them to take a moment to be aware of themselves too.

Unconscious Mirroring

As you learned above, conscious or unconscious copying another person is a powerful tool for increasing somatic empathy. You may remember that mirroring another person's facial expression, posture, or movement activates the same motor (mirror) neurons that fire in our brain as in theirs. As discussed, these cause an emotional and feeling response in the observer that matches the observed, often enabling a helping professional to literally feel what the person they are helping is feeling.

Being able to differentiate between which emotions and feelings belong to you and which belong to your client will enable you to know if you are vicariously feeling what your client is feeling, which is likely if you unconsciously mirror them, or if you are having a reaction of your own, possibly countertransference.

Did the earlier exercise, Notice Your Own Facial Expression, highlight for you that mirroring occurs unconsciously? When the timer went off, did you notice that your facial expression had changed? Such awareness can be essential to learning and connecting with one another and is usual when sharing normal ups and downs with family and friends. However, for helping professionals who are in contact with a greater than usual amount of distressed, traumatized, anxious, and depressed people, unconscious mirroring can cause serious problems.

Jamila felt not only the happiness of people she saw, such as the children playing in the park, but also the hopelessness of anyone she spent time with. Jamila's experiences of feeling the happiness and hopelessness of those she spent time with, is a good reminder that it is possible for mirrored feelings to be long lasting. Without our awareness, they can be presumed to be our own feelings, rather than a resonance with another's experience. That kind of confusion can sometimes cause serious difficulties.

> *When Jamila spoke to her supervisor about her experience with the children in the park, her supervisor asked if this was a common experience in her work. Jamila realized that she was not sure. She agreed to her supervisor's suggestion to take note of how she felt before and after each client as well as the emotion and feelings of her client. By tracking her emotional changes, Jamila would become able to identify which feelings were her own and which were mirrors of her clients'.*

| EXERCISE | Track Your Somatic Empathy |

It is advisable to do this exercise before and after one or more sessions over the next week.

1. Before a session, write down how you are currently feeling, including your posture, facial expression, mood, and emotion.
2. During the session, to the best of your ability, periodically bring your attention to both your and your client's posture, facial expression, mood, and emotion.
3. After the session, note the main feeling of your client during the session and any further observations about their posture, facial expression, and so on.
4. Next, notice your own facial expression, posture, mood, and feelings. Note if they are the same or different from the start of the session, and whether they are the same or different from your clients'.
5. At the end of the day, check your facial expression, posture, mood, and feelings again. Do any of those reflect one or more of the clients you saw earlier in the day, or perhaps the one you saw at the end of your day? If so, see if you can reconnect with your own feelings and mood by adjusting your posture and facial expression. That will reduce the chance of you, in essence, taking your client home with you.
6. Your somatic empathy likely changes depending on client, subject matter, time of day, your tiredness level, and countertransference. We shall discuss developing greater awareness of these further in Chapter 4.

Client name: _____

Observations about yourself before the session:

Mood _____

Body sensations _____

Facial expression _____

Posture _____

Emotions/feelings _____

Observations about the client:

Mood _____

Body sensations _____

Facial expression _____

Posture _____

Emotions/feelings _____

Observations about yourself after the session:

Mood _____

Body sensations _____

Facial expression _____

Posture _____

Emotions/feelings _____

Observations about yourself at the end of the day:

Mood _____

Body sensations _____

Facial expression _____

Posture _____

Emotions/feelings _____

Jamila discovered that she experienced stronger somatic empathy during and after the sessions with one client in particular. Her client Anne had very few friends and was feeling anxious and hopeless. Jamila wanted to connect with Anne and give her a real sense of relationship. She experienced greater attunement and connection when she mirrored Anne and was more able to understand and reflect Anne's experience. However, following the sessions, Jamila noticed that she too felt hopeless and anxious for the rest of the day, and sometimes those feelings continued for a few days.

Jamila's supervisor suggested that she gain greater awareness of her tendency to mirror and learn to control and reduce it. Jamila felt reluctant to do this. She did not want to reduce the feeling of attunement and the ability to understand her clients. She was worried she would come across as cold and distant. However, her supervisor felt that if she mirrored Anne with awareness, mirroring, and then consciously unmirroring, she would be able to offer the benefits of empathy while lowering the risks to her own and Anne's well-being. The supervisor wanted Jamila to be able to choose when and how much she attuned with Anne and her other clients.

The supervisor suggested they experiment with it in a supervision session rather than a client session. The supervisor told Jamila about a mildly stressful, but not traumatic, event that the supervisor had experienced over the weekend: She was in a rush to get to her friend's house for dinner but faced a long line at a store when she dropped by to quickly buy chocolates for dessert. Jamila mirrored the supervisor's facial expression and posture and found that she was able to get into contact with the stress the supervisor described. As the supervisor continued to speak about the experience, Jamila became increasingly drawn in by the story, so much so that when her supervisor asked how it was to mirror and unmirror, Jamila realized that she had completely forgotten to unmirror and noticed that her body posture mirrored that of her supervisor exactly. She was feeling the same tightness in her abdomen and slightly increased heart rate. Next, the supervisor suggested they do the same thing again, but with Jamila having a chance to focus on unmirroring and her own body awareness.

Awareness is key to gaining control of mirroring. In the process with her supervisor, Jamila realized that she easily became more engrossed in the story rather than holding awareness of both her client and herself; this is quite typical and will be further explored in Chapter 4. However, to gain control of mirroring, as with Jamila, your first step might be to explore whether you agree that being in control of unconscious mirroring and somatic empathy is useful. The exploration below may help to identify what works best for you.

EXERCISE   Concerns About Controlling Somatic Empathy

Like Jamila, decreasing empathy for clients might feel contradictory for you, because empathy is often something taught to and encouraged for helping professionals. It might be useful to notice any hesitations you may have with being in greater control of, and sometimes reducing, empathy with your clients. Knowing your viewpoint will help you to address when you feel it would and would not be useful to increase or decrease empathy, as well as to identify any support you may need in employing either approach in practice.

1. Note any reservations or concerns you have about reduced empathy with clients. Is there a client you are particularly concerned about this affecting?

_____

_____

_____

2. As with any therapeutic approach, it is important to consider its usefulness and when to employ it or not. There are many advantages to feeling empathy with those you work with, and disadvantages too. In the chart below, list how you see the positive and negative aspects of somatic empathy.

Advantages of somatic empathy	Disadvantages of somatic empathy

Your Personal Empathy Dial

Being in control of how much empathy you have for a client at any particular moment in time is essential for you to be an effective practitioner. It is possible to hold compassion and a desire to help and support clients without vicariously experiencing what they are experiencing. Most helping professionals do not need to learn to increase empathy for others, as that line of work generally attracts highly empathic people, yet many would benefit from being more in control of their empathy and how deeply they resonate with others.

In the revised edition of *Help for the Helper*, Babette described the use of an empathy dial to help develop awareness of the level of empathy you feel for the person you are working with (Rothschild, 2022). She described imagining a dial that you can adjust to control the amount of empathy you have for a client: "Turning it up means you resonate stronger emotionally, somatically, and intuitively. Turning it down will give you increased emotional and energetic distance, making objectivity and clearer thinking more possible" (Rothschild, 2022).

EXERCISE   Empathy Dial

1. Draw, visualize, or find an image for a dial, like the ones you find on volume or brightness control on a mobile phone or television, or the volume dial on a stereo. For example:

2. Think of the dial as representing degrees of empathy for a client.
3. Check in with this empathy dial throughout sessions, and outside sessions if you notice you are thinking about a client or making decisions about their treatment and balancing your self-care. Mark your empathy level on the dial in the chart below.

Activity	Empathy level
e.g., Discussing financial pressures, last client on a Thursday afternoon	

4. List the ways that having your dial too high in some situations could be problematic.

_____

_____

_____

_____

_____

5. List the ways that having your dial too low in some situations could be problematic.

_____

_____

_____

_____

_____

Unmirroring

As discussed, because mirroring somatic expression causes an emotional response, it is useful for therapists to be in control of it. Feeling the same overwhelm, anxiety, sadness, or rage as your clients is unlikely to be useful. Rather more useful would be to maintain calm, clear thinking and present awareness, which, in turn, may be mirrored by clients, enabling them to be calmer and more present too. It is much better for the client to mirror the calm therapist than for the therapist to mirror the overwhelmed client.

Again, self-awareness is key to noticing if you are mirroring unconsciously. Noticing your and the client's posture and facial expression, and noticing your mood and body sensations and feelings can enable you to be aware of whether or not you are mirroring your client.

If you are, the next step would be to unmirror, that is, to consciously change your position, breathing rate, or facial expression to be different from your client's. This does not need to be obvious or extreme. It might be that if your client was crying, your mouth might be straight rather than downturned. If you notice both you and your client have crossed legs, you might put your feet flat on the floor. If you notice both you and your client are leaning toward each other, you might sit back in your chair.

EXERCISE   Unmirror With a Mirror

1. Watch a television program or movie with a mirror nearby.
2. As in the previous exercise, you could set an alarm to sound every few minutes so that you can catch yourself unaware.
3. At the sound of the alarm, pause the movie and look in the mirror. Notice if your facial expression and posture mimic what you see on screen. If so, change your expression. Check in the mirror to experiment with a facial expression that feels appropriate but not mirroring.
   For example, if Winona Ryder is looking sad on screen, with frowning mouth, furrowed brow, and head in hands, changing your facial expression to a beaming smile might not be an appropriate response to transfer to client work. However, looking in the mirror to experiment with a facial expression without a downturned mouth, and with a relaxed forehead, would likely still be appropriate but not triggering the somatic markers for you to feel sadness.

4. Experiment with different facial expressions and postures in the mirror to get a sense of how different facial expressions feel and look. Aim for compassion without the somatic markers of powerful feelings.

EXERCISE Unmirroring With Friends and Colleagues

Gaining confidence and self-awareness by practicing unmirroring with friends and colleagues is useful before trying it with clients.

1. You might do several experiments both formally and informally. Just talking in the course of a normal day with friends and family gives plenty of opportunity for practice. However, you might also partner up with a friend or colleague, explain the exercise to them, and both of you try it out, switching roles periodically.

2. As you listen, experiment with unmirroring. If the other person leans forward, feel the back of your chair rather than leaning forward. If they smile, keep a gentle expression but not a full smile. If you notice both of you have feet flat on the floor, maybe cross your ankles. Don't worry if it sometimes feels a little like the game Simon Says, as though you change and the other person changes to match you, or vice versa.

3. Notice how it feels not to mirror. It may feel unnatural or unusual to start with, which is why it is a good idea to practice.

4. Again, as you listen, consciously move between mirroring and unmirroring. As you listen to what they are talking about, notice any pull to get distracted by their story or any increased pull to mirror.

EXERCISE Somatic Markers Connected With Current Clients

Being aware of your usual responses with your clients can prepare you to be in control of somatic empathy and mirroring. In this exercise you are invited to remember sitting with each of your clients and then to notice your response.

1. First, use the Mindful Check-In exercise to pay attention to your current mood, posture, and so on.

2. For each client, one at a time, remember your last session together. Remember where and how you each sat, how you interacted, and the content of your conversation.

3. As you recall the conversation, notice your response right now—are there any changes?

　　Client ID _____

　　Posture _____

　　Facial expression _____

　　Mood/emotions _____

　　ANS response _____

4. As you remember the client session, note your own current:

　　Posture _____

　　Facial expression _____

　　Mood/emotions _____

　　ANS response _____

5. Remember the session with your client, but this time maintain your own current posture and facial expression, not a mirror of the client's. How do you feel?

Controlling Imagery

Controlling images in your mind is another aspect of empathy control that is essential, particularly when working with clients who are telling you about their traumatic events or sharing difficult experiences. The first key step to this is, again, present moment awareness,. If you notice yourself imagining (in pictures, sounds, or sensations in your body) what is being said or described, stop yourself immediately. This is unlikely to assist you in being present and calm for your clients; moreover, it could lead to vicarious traumatization.

Imagining something terrible that happened to another through visual, auditory, or sensory images drives up the empathy dial to its highest point, making you much more vulnerable to vicarious trauma. In your body and mind, such imagery might seem as if the event happened to you or that you witnessed it firsthand. This is not an advantage for helping your client and could be very risky for your own emotional well-being.

Samuel enjoyed swimming and had even competed in freestyle when he was younger. However, lately, when he walked to the local pool his heart started pounding and his mouth would go dry. He thought maybe he was drinking too much coffee, but cutting back did not change anything, and he was starting to dread walking to what once was his favorite relaxation activity. But it was when the recurring nightmares of drowning started that Samuel realized he needed some help. His supervisor, figuring that Samuel was recovering a childhood memory, recommended a few trauma therapy sessions. However, after taking a careful history, the therapist concluded differently, as there was no such trauma in his history. The cause of Samuel's anxiety, dread, and nightmares turned out to be vicarious trauma. A recent client had survived near drowning in a tsunami a decade ago. Samuel had forgotten that as the client recounted her experience, he had been automatically imagining what it must have been like for her. Even though those images would periodically intrude when he was not working with that client, he did not mind, as he was hoping to better understand her trauma symptoms. Nevertheless, in doing so, Samuel had not realized that her terrifying experience was actually becoming imprinted on his own nervous system as if it had happened to him.

EXERCISE   Stop Imagining Disturbing Images in Your Mind

1. The first important step is developing mindful self-awareness. Use the Mindful Check-In exercise in this chapter a few times a day, when you are both with and not with clients, to build a habit of doing so. This will greatly increase your likelihood of noticing that you are seeing, hearing, or feeling images of what your client is telling you. Awareness will make it possible for you to stop yourself.

2. It may be necessary to develop a firm adult internal "voice" to be compassionate but firm with yourself about this. There are some steps here that may help with this, but you may also wish to develop it with support from your supervisor if you find this difficult.

3. List reasons you can think of as to why you feel that it is not a good idea to imagine disturbing scenes you are told about. Next list any reasons it might be a good idea.

It is not a good idea to imagine a disturbing scene because . . .	It is a good idea to imagine a disturbing scene because . . .

Imagery Control

It may be that you have already imagined something a client has told you, and it replays in your mind, or that a lapse in awareness caused you to visualize something you would like to gain control of. The first step is to practice image control using an image that is neutral or pleasant. That way you will be more able to stay present and calm as you gain confidence in your ability to manipulate and control the images in your mind. Images can be pictures, sounds, smells, tastes, or any combination, and they can also be imagined body sensations. Notice which are predominant for you and experiment with gaining control of one at a time. The exercises below focus on control of visual and auditory images; however, you can use the same principles to gain control of any of the other types of images.

EXERCISE Controlling Visual Images

1. Take your time, perhaps a minute or so, with each of these.
   a. Begin by imagining a blue ball floating in the air or lying on the floor.
   b. Change the imagined ball's color to red.
   c. Increase its size.
   d. Change its color to orange.
   e. Change it into a basketball.
   f. Change it to an orange balloon.
   g. Imagine it losing air and getting smaller and smaller until all the air is out, and it is a deflated balloon.

2. Now try these.
   a. Imagine a cube with polka dots, color of your choice.
   b. Turn its spots to a different color.
   c. Increase its size.
   d. Imagine it warps into a pyramid.
   e. Change the color to purple.
   f. Imagine the pyramid shrinking in size until it is just a tiny dot.
   g. Now choose your own imagined object, changing size, color, and so on as above.

3. Notice if anything helps you to imagine the changes.
   For example, closing your eyes, keeping your eyes open, sitting down, standing up:

   _____

   _____

   _____

   _____

4. When you feel proficient, experiment with the memory image of a *minor* stress such as waiting in traffic or having a minor conflict at work. Play it in your mind like a movie or video.

5. Change distinct parts of the image one at a time; for example, change the video to black and white or sepia, stop it and start it again, make it bigger, make it smaller, change the location, such as from a street to a beach; change a person to a famous actor.

EXERCISE Blur the Image

Back to imagining a ball, but this time, imagine looking at it through a camera lens.

1. Imagine bringing the ball into and out of focus so that it goes from being clear to blurred, and then back and forth between clear and blurred.
2. Next, imagine blurring the background of the ball.
3. Imagine blurring just the ball.
4. Shift between blurry background with focused ball and the opposite, blurry ball, and focused background.
5. Again, when you feel proficient with this, try each of these steps out, first on an image of a minor stress.
6. When you feel confident with these exercises, you may be ready to use the same procedures to experiment with this technique on any unwanted imagery.

EXERCISE Auditory Images

As with the previous exercises, start first with a sound that is not disturbing to you. Once you feel proficient, experiment with sounds of minor stress before experimenting with disturbing auditory images. This may be useful if you have a critical inner voice.

1. Imagine you have a remote control for a music player. Imagine the different buttons for volume, play, fast forward, rewind, pause.
2. Bring to mind a song or tune that you like.
3. Use your imaginary remote control to rewind a bit.
4. Next speed it up a little.
5. Slow it down.
6. Make it louder, make it softer.
7. Change the singer's voice to a cartoon character of your choice.
8. Mute every other word of the song.
9. Turn down the volume so it is barely audible.

CHAPTER 3

Keeping Calm

Most trauma therapists monitor their client's *autonomic nervous system* (ANS) for somatic signs of fight, flight, freeze, calm, and lethargy so that they can help them to manage and integrate the therapy. However, many therapists do not give that same attention to their own ANS changes during sessions with clients. The therapist's ability to track and develop self-awareness is imperative for their own well-being, to prevent vicarious trauma and compassion fatigue, and also to be able to stay calm, present, and clear-thinking with their distressed client.

THE AUTONOMIC NERVOUS SYSTEM

The updated and expanded edition of *Help for the Helper* includes a six-column table that represents the array of ANS states that are possible in both calm and stressful circumstances (Rothschild, 2022). Each described state highlights the somatic, emotional, cognitive, and relational differences likely to be observed or experienced in each. We encourage you to refer to that text if you would like to see the table or read an in-depth theoretical explanation. Here we will avoid the scientific jargon, keep the theoretical discussion brief, and tie it to tools for improving your self-care and preventing vicarious trauma and compassion fatigue.

Normal activation refers to levels consistent with non-life-threatening daily life. Levels of activation may go up and down a bit depending on the level of stimulation, for example, reading a pleasant book versus hurrying to meet a deadline. However, in the normal range there is nothing that would be associated with life-threat. Normal activation includes a range of somatic, emotional, cognitive, and relational differences. For example, while quietly drinking a cup of tea in the garden, respiration and heart rate may be steady and slower than compared with resolving a conflict or having sex. In this state, integration, relational contact, and present awareness are likely all possible.

Heightened activation refers to levels of activation associated with an actual or perceived threat to life or bodily integrity and include the well-known responses to trauma: fight, flight, and freeze. During fight or flight activation, somatic responses can include muscle tension, increased heart rate and respiration, feelings of rage and fear, and reduced or lack of ability for relational contact, integration, and present awareness. If fight/flight is not possible, it can lead to increased activation of one of two ranges of freeze responses. *Hyper-freeze,* similar to a deer or kangaroo caught in headlights, is characterized by rigid muscles and very fast respiration and heart rate. In contrast, *hypo-freeze* is like a mouse that plays dead when attacked by a cat, reacting with flaccid muscles and extremely slow respiration and heart rate, which can become life-threatening if prolonged.

Lethargic activation refers to levels of activation lower than would normally be expected. This may be associated with depression or emotions such as grief, shame, and disgust. A person in lethargic activation may be withdrawn, with little capacity for social interaction or cognitive integration.

Illustrating the Brain à la Dan Siegel

Daniel Siegel's (2010) Hand Model of the Brain is one of the handiest (pun intended) tools you can have for understanding the basics of how the brain functions under stress. It is best to follow the description with your own hand as you read it and to repeat it at least a couple of times.

Using your hand to represent your brain, hold your hand in front of you, palm facing toward you. Your wrist represents the position of your spinal cord, the heel of your hand your brain stem, the palm of your hand the limbic system, and your fingers, the cortex. When you fold your thumb over into the palm of your hand, that approximates the position of the limbic system's hippocampus, and your thumbnail approximates the position of the amygdala. When you fold your fingers over your thumb, the first knuckles of your fingers represent your prefrontal cortex.

When you are in a calm state, the "thinking brain," the prefrontal cortex, is online and in communication with the other parts of the brain. This part of your brain enables you to problem-solve, plan, imagine, and analyze.

When your nervous system is activated into stressful states, you can lose connection to your frontal cortex, represented by a lifting of the fingers away from the thumb, like a "flipped lid." In that state, you are controlled more by your emotional brain, and clear thinking is not available.

Understanding the impact of arousal on your ability to think clearly will help you, for example, with a client who is triggered and has flipped their lid. That is often activating for a therapist, as we explored in Chapter 2. It is essential that you are able to keep your lid on at all times to prevent vicarious trauma and compassion fatigue, and maintain your professional competency. This chapter will provide you with tools, including mindful self-awareness and self-observation of your ANS state, to enable you to lower your activation and avoid flipping your lid.

MONITORING YOUR ANS ACTIVATION LEVEL

Mindful Self-Awareness

> *Ursula was in a rush to get her children to school before she had to be at work for an appointment with a client. Rather than getting their socks and shoes on, as she had requested, they continued to paint. When they persisted, Ursula uncharacteristically raised her voice, shouting at the children to stop what they were doing and put on their shoes. When the youngest started to cry, Ursula realized that she had been more sharp than usual and had actually flipped her lid. She took a minute to mindfully check in with herself and noticed she was feeling a little dizzy, her heart rate had increased, and she was feeling frustrated. She remembered some things that helped when she felt like this: She drank a glass of cold water, wiggled her toes, and sighed a deep exhale. Lid back on, she then reconnected with the children, repaired the argument, and helped them to put their shoes on and get out the door.*
>
> *Arriving at work a few minutes late, Ursula found she was still feeling a little of the ANS activation from earlier. Her first client was jittery and spoke very quickly. Ursula, continuing to mindfully monitor herself, instantly noticed her own ANS respond, again feeling a little dizzy and her heart rate quicken. She took a sip of cold water, wiggled her toes, and employed strategies to unmirror her client (see Chapter 2). She noticed her breath becoming deeper and her heart rate slowing, and she felt calmer and more in control.*

Applications of mindfulness are many and varied. In this workbook, we refer to mindfulness as the practice of awareness of the present moment. This can include awareness of your body using your exteroceptive and interoceptive senses, emotions, and thoughts.

In the example above, Ursula was empowered by her self-awareness. While she did feel overwhelmed and had lost her temper, she was able to be aware of what had happened with her children and what would help her to reduce the unwelcome activation. The first step to taking control is to have good awareness of your individual signs of ANS activation as well as what helps you in those states. Ursula noticed a variety of physical sensations that indicated ANS activation had increased: Body awareness is key to recognizing ANS activation.

The following exercises are created with both those who are experienced with practicing mindful awareness and those who are new to it in mind. Feel free to approach each exercise at your own level and pace, tweaking the instructions to suit your own needs.

EXERCISE   Self Check-In

Creating a regular practice of checking in with your body sensations, emotions, and thoughts can develop a habit that offers a great deal of information about yourself as well as the opportunity to better your self-care. For example, simply taking a moment to notice your current ANS levels gives you self-knowledge and provides opportunity to stick with or change your state as you want to.

Ursula had not recognized the bodily and emotional indicators that she was about to flip her lid. If she had developed a habit of regularly checking in, she may have seen it coming and been able to use some of her resources and regain a sense of calm before the situation escalated. However, now that she has become aware of what happened with her children, she is in a better position to be on the lookout for a similar pattern of emotional and body signals in the future.

On your workdays, you might choose to check in at a particular time throughout the day, such as 10 minutes before the hour, or you might set an alarm on your cell phone to sound or vibrate every 45 minutes, or maybe connect the check-in with a part of your routine, such as before each client, or while waiting for the kettle to boil. Experiment to find out what works well for you.

Feel free to experiment and approach these exercises in any order that works best for you and skip those that do not appeal. The first exercise is simply about noticing, not about trying to change anything. It may be useful to write down what you notice in the chart below, or in your journal, so that you can keep track of what you observe.

The more times you practice checking in, the quicker each check-in will become, and the easier it will be to remember to do it. Once you feel adept, you might try during a session with a client, possibly when you invite your client to do the same. You may or may not decide to share that you are checking in with yourself, depending on your relationship with the client and their needs.

The exercises below are designed to help you to increase your ability for mindful awareness in various situations and with different stimuli. Feel free to adjust one or more to be the most useful to you and skip any that don't appeal.

1. Observation Only Body Check-In

Caveat: Some readers will find it pleasant to go through this entire exercise at one time. However, for others, that could be overwhelming. Take this at your own pace. Perhaps focusing on just one body part or just a few is a big enough portion. The value will be in increasing your awareness of yourself, not in trying to do it all at once. Feel free to return to this exercise as often (or not) as you would like for whatever portion fits you.

a. Move your awareness through your body bit by bit, simply noticing any sensations. Take a moment or so with each body part to notice any sensations. You might notice pain, or lack of pain, numbness, tingling, muscle tensing, muscles relaxed, aching, or no ache.

b. One at a time, notice sensations that are and are not present in that moment in that part of your body.

- left foot
- right foot
- left ankle
- right ankle
- left lower leg
- right lower leg
- left knee
- right knee
- left upper leg
- right upper leg
- sit bones
- pelvis
- hips
- abdomen
- chest
- back and spine
- left arm and hand
- right arm and hand
- neck
- face
- back of your head
- top of your head

c. Using the diagram below, draw a line from the body part and describe any sensation you notice there, possibly using some of the suggested vocabulary: tight;

soft; lengthened; faster; slow; fidgety; stiff; numb; deep; shallow; cold; steady; painful; aching; warm; sweaty. Make sure to add your own descriptive vocabulary as you discover it.

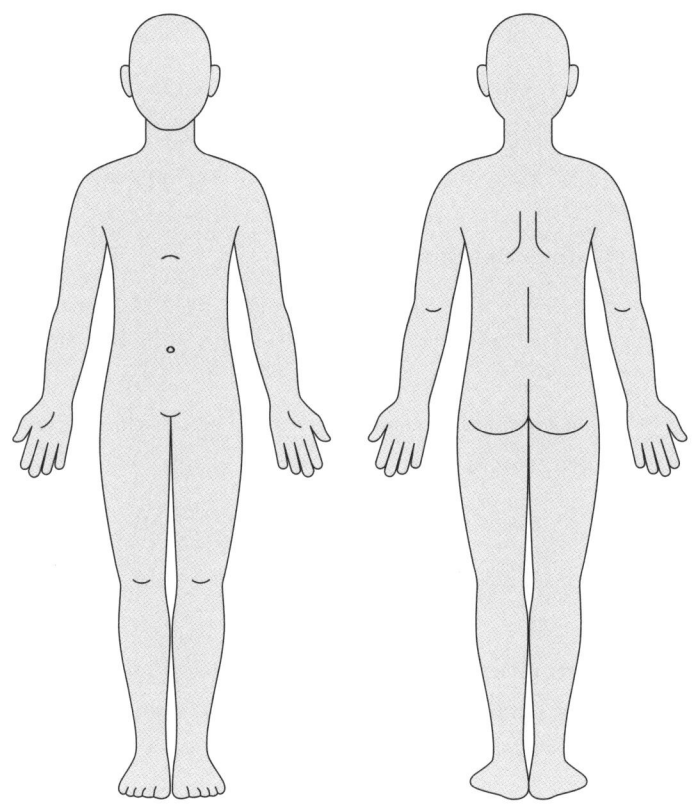

2. Emotion and Mood Check-In

Notice what emotion or mood you are feeling right now.

For example, angry / sad / afraid / worried / tired / happy / frustrated / nervous

_____

_____

3. Thoughts Check-In

a. Notice the quality and content of your thoughts.

b. Are different thoughts racing through your mind, jumping to different things, or do you feel focused and easily able to concentrate, or do your thoughts feel sluggish or stuck?

c. Are your thoughts about the present, past, or future?

d. Are your thoughts encouraging, pragmatic, or critical?

e. Qualities of thoughts, such as sluggish, difficult to think; lots of thoughts moving rapidly and difficult to hold on to one thought.

_____

_____

_____

f. Content of thoughts: For example, I cannot do it; I love the . . . ; I hate the . . . ; This reminds me of . . . ; I wish it were . . .

_____

_____

_____

EXERCISE Mindful Eating to Notice Your Responses

Before fully assessing your own responses in different ANS states, you can begin to mindfully notice changes in your body in relation to various stimuli.

1. Choose a food stimulus. This might be something you already know will provoke a reaction, though *not* a trigger of trauma.
   For example, a pleasant stimulus might be chocolate or fruit. A less pleasant stimulus might be the taste of something you don't like. Of course, do not experiment with any foods that cause allergies or intolerance.

2. Look at the food in front of you and notice any change in body sensation, thought, or emotion.

3. Smell the piece of food, breathing in the aroma a few times. Notice any physical, thought, or emotional response.

4. Put the food item in your mouth, and hold it in your mouth before chewing it. Notice any physical, thought, or emotional response.

5. Start to chew the food. Notice any physical, thought, or emotional response.

6. After you have swallowed the food, notice the aftertaste. Notice any physical, thought, or emotional response.

7. Experiment with foods you like a lot and foods you don't like so much.

Food stimulus:

1._____ 2. _____

    1. Usually pleasant / usually unpleasant (circle)

    2. Usually pleasant / usually unpleasant (circle)

Physical, thought, or emotional response as you look at the food.

1._____ 2. _____

Physical, thought, or emotional response as you smell the food.

1._____ 2. _____

Physical, thought, or emotional response as you hold the food in your mouth.

1._____ 2. _____

Physical, thought, or emotional response as you chew.

1._____ 2. _____

Physical, thought, or emotional response with the aftertaste.

1._____ 2. _____

EXERCISE   Mindful Shifting to Notice Your Responses

Shifting between a pleasant and unpleasant response can heighten your awareness of how you respond to each.

> *When Mai looks at a photograph of her beloved dog, she notices a gentle smile, warmth in her chest and belly, softening of her shoulders, a spontaneous sighing breath, and a lift in her mood. If she then looks at an image of a to-do list, her face falls a little, and she notices more tension in her chest and arms, a slight increase in heart rate, and a feeling of worry. Looking back at the image of her dog, she hears her sighing exhale, feels a sense of relief and joy, and her shoulder muscles soften. The response to each seems more pronounced as they fall at opposite ends of a continuum of pleasant and unpleasant.*

1. Choose two images or objects to look at, smell, or feel, that you already have a sense are pleasant and unpleasant to you. These should *not* be in any way

attached to a trauma memory or cause you to feel overwhelmed; aim for mildly unpleasant.

Stimulus:

Pleasant: _____ Unpleasant: _____

2. Bring your awareness to the pleasant stimulus and notice any responses from your body, mind, or emotions. These might be subtle, instant, potent, or take a moment to generate. Make a note of your responses below.

Physical, thought, or emotional response to the pleasant stimulus:

_____

3. Now let that go and focus on the unpleasant stimulus. Notice any responses, and note them below.

Physical, thought, or emotional response to the unpleasant stimulus:

_____

4. Shift your attention back to the pleasant stimulus, again noticing your responses, and then back to the unpleasant one.

Physical, thought, or emotional response to the pleasant stimulus:

_____

Physical, thought, or emotional response to the unpleasant stimulus:

_____

5. End the exercise by noticing your response to the pleasant stimulus, noting your responses.

Physical, thought, or emotional response to the pleasant stimulus:

_____

Mindful Self-Awareness in the Therapy Room

Ursula used the exercises above to develop mindful awareness of her own responses to stimuli and became confident about recognizing unpleasant and pleasant responses. She used her new skills throughout her day to notice how her responses to things could help inform her decisions, such as noticing what she preferred to wear that day and when her wife asked if she wanted to go out to the theater or the movies. She noticed her bodily responses to each option, and this helped her to decide that she would prefer to go to the movies.

Ursula's awareness practice paid off. When her boss asked if she would like to take on an additional client, she was ready to gauge her response. She checked in with herself about each option: an increase in her workload and the increase in pay compared with the same workload and pay. On another day, when a client emailed to ask if they could swap their session time to later in the day than planned, Ursula was able to check in with her response to assist in identifying how she felt about doing that. She noticed a sudden sense of weariness, her mouth turned down at the sides, and her heart rate quickened a little. She decided that she did not want to work late and offered a different time to her client that better suited herself.

As for Ursula, it may be a good idea for you to practice mindful awareness in your day-to-day life. Evaluate if or how it assists you in making choices which are helpful in your everyday life, as well as professionally. Include areas such as choosing which self-care strategy would be best in a particular moment, or when responding to questions or requests from colleagues or clients.

| EXERCISE | Noticing Your Response While Having Awareness of Something Else: Part 1 |

Like Ursula, you may feel it would be useful to practice checking in with your own responses at the same time as being aware of someone or something else. A radio or television program can be useful to develop this skill. Similar to the previous exercise, in this exercise you will experiment with shifting your awareness between your responses and the program.

This exercise and the ones that follow are also good opportunities to pay attention to how easily you get absorbed in a story and lose awareness of yourself. They provide a safe place to learn to turn down your empathy dial so you can both actually listen and simultaneously pay mindful attention to yourself.

1. Choose a television or radio program, ideally one that includes talking and will not be too stressful, such as a cooking or travel program.

   Program: _____

2. Prepare a timer to sound or vibrate at an interval that is comfortable for you, perhaps every 2 minutes over a 10-minute period.

3. To begin, notice any current body sensations, mood or emotions, and thoughts, and jot them down below.

4. Start the timer and start watching the program.

5. Each time the timer goes off, notice your body sensations, thoughts, emotions, or mood.

     Your responses:

     a. _____

     b. _____

     c. _____

     d. _____

     e. _____

     f. _____

     g. _____

     h. _____

     i. _____

     j. _____

6. Once you feel comfortable with switching back and forth between noticing the program and noting your own responses, the next step is to experiment with keeping an awareness of what is being said on the program at the same time as being self-aware. For most people, this will take time and several trials to get good at this and gain confidence in your ability.

EXERCISE Noticing Your Response While Having Awareness of Something Else: Part 2

Once you have developed the first step of shifting your awareness between the program and your own responses, experiment with different genres to gain more information about your responses to different emotions, such as: What are your usual responses to love stories, to sad scenes, to comedy, to action, to something a little scary?

Being able to identify your subtle responses to emotions and how you experience them in your body will help you to identify them when you are in the therapy room. Identifying the subtle signs for each emotion means that you are more able to recognize them and resource yourself, hopefully preventing risk of flipping your lid.

1. Do the same procedure as the previous exercise, this time choosing specific scenes from a movie (YouTube can be useful for short movie scenes) that are a particular genre or invoke a particular emotion.

   We have some suggestions below to get you started thinking about emotional movie scenes, but these are highly subjective depending on one's own tastes, life experience, and generation. So make sure to choose a movie scene according to your personal responses rather than ours.

   Sad
   - *Little Women*: When Beth dies
   - *Frozen*: Olaf's death
   - *For Colored Girls*: Crystal scrubbing the sidewalk
   - *E.T.*: When E.T. goes home

   Happy
   - *Dirty Dancing*: When Johnny asks Baby to dance at the end-of-year show
   - *Matilda*: When the pupils get their revenge on Miss Trunchbull
   - *The Blues Brothers*: Police car chase
   - *The Pursuit of Happiness*: Chris is hired

   Angry
   - *Pride and Prejudice*: When Darcy lists the reasons it is irrational to love Lizzie
   - *The Lion King*: When Mufasa is killed
   - *Philadelphia*: When Andrew is fired

   Afraid
   - *The Witches*: When the Grand High Witch turns Luke into a mouse
   - *Fried Green Tomatoes*: When Frank Bennett and Ruth return to get her belongings

2. Choose a scene from the list above or one of your own that you believe will provoke a particular emotion:

   _____

3. Set a timer to sound every minute.

4. Start the scene and the timer, and every time the timer goes off, notice your body sensations and emotions. You may initially need to pause the scene while you check in with yourself.

5. After watching the scene, again notice your response. Make a note of your responses to each emotion below. Include the very subtle responses as well as the more explicit ones.

> *When watching the very sad scene in* For Colored Girls *where Crystal is scrubbing the sidewalk, Ursula notices first a tightness in her chest and a little stuffiness in the top of her nasal passageway. Then her eyebrows move toward each other, her mouth turns downward, she feels prickles in her eyes, her nostrils flare a little, and eventually tears roll down her face.*

Possible Responses to Sad Scenes

Possible body sensations	Tight chest	Soft belly	Lengthened spine	Heart beating faster	Fidgety
	Feeling stiff	Numb	Soft eyes	Sighing	Holding your breath
	Soft muscles	Cold	Heart beating steadily	Pain/aching	Sweaty
	Warm	Smiling	Frowning	Eyebrows move together	Holding your breath
Quality of thoughts	Racing, lots of different topics	Focus and concentrate on what I choose	Sluggish, not shifting		
Possible thoughts	I cannot do it	I love the . . .	I hate it	This reminds me of . . .	I wish it were . . .
	I do not like . . .	I am glad it is . . .	I prefer . . .	I do not understand . . .	

Possible Responses to Happy Scenes

Possible body sensations	Tight chest	Soft belly	Lengthened spine	Heart beating faster	Fidgety
	Feeling stiff	Numb	Soft eyes	Sighing	Holding your breath
	Soft muscles	Cold	Heart beating steadily	Pain/aching	Sweaty
	Warm	Smiling	Frowning	Eyebrows move together	Holding your breath
Quality of thoughts	Racing, lots of different topics	Focus and concentrate on what I choose	Sluggish, not shifting		
Possible thoughts	I cannot do it	I love the . . .	I hate it	This reminds me of . . .	I wish it were . . .
	I do not like . . .	I am glad it is . . .	I prefer . . .	I do not understand . . .	

Possible Responses to Angry Scenes

Possible body sensations	Tight chest	Soft belly	Lengthened spine	Heart beating faster	Fidgety
	Feeling stiff	Numb	Soft eyes	Sighing	Holding your breath
	Soft muscles	Cold	Heart beating steadily	Pain/aching	Sweaty
	Warm	Smiling	Frowning	Eyebrows move together	Holding your breath
Quality of thoughts	Racing, lots of different topics	Focus and concentrate on what I choose	Sluggish, not shifting		
Possible thoughts	I cannot do it	I love the . . .	I hate it	This reminds me of . . .	I wish it were . . .
	I do not like . . .	I am glad it is . . .	I prefer . . .	I do not understand . . .	

Possible Responses to Scary Scenes

Possible body sensations	Tight chest	Soft belly	Lengthened spine	Heart beating faster	Fidgety
	Feeling stiff	Numb	Soft eyes	Sighing	Holding your breath
	Soft muscles	Cold	Heart beating steadily	Pain/aching	Sweaty
	Warm	Smiling	Frowning	Eyebrows move together	Holding your breath
Quality of thoughts	Racing, lots of different topics	Focus and concentrate on what I choose	Sluggish, not shifting		
Possible thoughts	I cannot do it	I love the . . .	I hate it	This reminds me of . . .	I wish it were . . .
	I do not like . . .	I am glad it is . . .	I prefer . . .	I do not understand . . .	

EXERCISE   Check-In Reminders

How is it for you to use a timer to remind yourself to check in? Is this something you would like to continue to do? What are other ways you could remind yourself it is time for a check-in?

A timer or other agreed-upon strategy can be used in sessions with clients too. Many of our clients appreciate having an interval timer to check in with body sensations and emotions. Just as it can be helpful to you, it can also be useful to your clients to practice in the moment so they will be better able to do it outside the therapy room. You can do your check-in at the same time and decide whether or not it is therapeutically appropriate to share that you are doing it too.

It may be useful to consider other ways to remind you to check in, in case a timer is not available or is not appropriate, such as in a job interview.

List possible ways you can remember to self-check-in:

• Keep an eye on the clock and check in every couple of minutes.

- Every time you notice a change in the person you are speaking with, check in with yourself.
- Every time there is a change in topic of the conversation, check in.
- Continually shift between noticing the other person and noticing yourself.

- _____
- _____
- _____
- _____
- _____
- _____
- _____
- _____
- _____

EXERCISE Self-Awareness in Conversation

The next step towards being able to hold self-awareness in sessions with clients is to practice with a friend, partner, or colleague. We recommend that you start with speaking about something that doesn't tend to provoke any stressful response from you. We have made some suggestions for topics below. Once you have got the hang of shifting between noticing your partner, checking in with yourself, and experimenting with doing both at the same time, the final practice step would be to experiment with your partner sharing a very mildly stressful event from the past 24 hours.

1. Choose a partner and explain the exercises. This might be useful to do with a colleague, who can then swap roles so that they can develop their self-awareness too. However, this is a skill that can be useful for everyone, so a friend or partner would also be good.

2. Choose a non-stressful topic for your partner to speak about, maybe their favorite memory of being at a beach, or their favorite flavor of ice cream and when they last ate it, or telling you about something they enjoyed last weekend.
   - Set a timer to sound every 30 seconds during the next 3 minutes.
   - Ask your partner to start talking and whenever the timer sounds, check in with your responses.

3. When the 3 minutes are over, start the task again, this time without the timer, checking in with yourself often.
   - Invite your partner to start talking again, possibly speaking about a different pleasant topic. Set an alarm to go off in 3 minutes to signal a stop in the exercise.
   - This time, as you are listening, shift your awareness between noticing them, noticing yourself, noticing them, noticing yourself.
4. Reflect on which method was most effective.
5. Next, invite your partner to consider a mildly stressful event from the past 24 hours, possibly along the lines of having to wait in a long line at the store, or rain starting as they set off on their bicycle to work, or noticing they were out of milk for their morning coffee.
6. Repeat the steps above for the mildly stressful event. Assess whether it is easier for you with a timer sounding or whether shifting between each of you is possible.
7. Next practice the same, but without the timer. Experiment with strategies to help you remember to check in with yourself.
8. Once you feel comfortable, start to use the same strategy in sessions with clients.
9. Make a note of what helped you to remember to check in with yourself and what happened when you forgot to.

EXERCISE Self-Observation of ANS State

In the previous exercises, we have explored emotional responses that are within the calm ANS state. The next step is to use your body awareness skills to notice the state of your ANS at any point in time. Differentiating between different states (for example: between calm and stressed, having a flipped lid or being just about to flip your lid, and so on) can be essential to regaining control and eventually calming your ANS so you can get your lid back on and think clearly again.

EXERCISE Your Calm

Having a clear map of what calm feels like can help you assess whether or not you are feeling it and when you are straying from it. This exercise will help you to identify what calm is for you.

A calm state can feel different for different people and in response to various situations. For example, if Ursula had recognized starting to feel hot and angry, she may have been able to use her resources to stay calm enough to hold the boundary with her children without losing her temper. It may also be useful to note that staying calm under pressure is a different type (or feeling) of calm than the calm you might feel relaxing at a spa.

1. First, to help you connect with a calm feeling, recall a pleasant memory when you were calm. It might be recent or in the past.
2. Bring everything about that memory to mind, remembering what you saw, felt, heard, smelled, and/or tasted.
3. As you elicit that memory, notice if you can remember your body sensations, posture, and thoughts. Also check in and notice if the body sensations and thoughts you are experiencing right now correspond with a feeling of calm.
4. You may want to add to the table below what you notice the next time you feel calm.
5. Repeat the same for two or three more memories of calm to see if you recognize a range of responses that indicate calm for you, as in the two examples of Ursula above.

What calm feels like for me	
Body sensations	
Posture	
Quality of thoughts	
Content of thoughts	

EXERCISE Your Activated ANS

The purpose of this exercise is to explore your individual physical and emotional responses in various states of ANS activation so that you are better equipped to recognize and respond to stay in control.

Do not experiment with a traumatic event for this exercise; we are not aiming for (nor do we want) you to flip your lid. The aim is for you to notice the subtle signs of stress activation. You may have already gathered information from previous times when you have flipped your lid, and it will be useful to add what you can remember of those responses. For example, when Ursula had calmed down, she still remembered how hot she had felt just before she lost her temper.

1. Recall a slightly stressful incident that took place in the last 48 hours. For example, having to wait in line at the store, being stuck in a traffic jam, or getting a puncture on your bicycle tire.
2. Bring everything about that memory to mind, remembering everything you saw, felt, heard, smelled, and/or tasted.
3. As you elicit that memory, notice if you can remember your body sensations, posture, and thoughts. Also check in and notice the body sensations and thoughts you are experiencing right now. Do any correspond with a feeling of ANS stress activation?
4. Noticing these responses will give you a sense of what your own stress response feels like so that you are able to identify and track it more easily.
5. Repeat the same for two or three more memories of ANS stress activation to see if you recognize a range of responses that indicate activation for you.

What stress-activated ANS feels like for me	
Body sensations	
Posture	
Quality of thoughts	
Content of thoughts	

Monitoring ANS Activation

Ursula identified signs when she was about to flip her lid: She felt agitated, short-tempered, her feet and chest felt hot, her legs and hands were fidgety, a little twitchy, and tense, her heart rate increased, her thoughts became erratic, lots of different thoughts flitted through her mind making it hard to focus, and it was difficult to make eye contact with others.

When she felt calm, with her lid firmly on, she found it easy to breathe, her muscles were toned but not tense, she could focus and make decisions easily, and she was not twitchy or fidgety. She found it easy to make eye contact with people.

Ursula tracked her ANS levels each day for a couple of weeks.

MONDAY

ANS activation/ flipped lid									
Starting to feel ANS activation	X	X							
Calm			X	X	X	X	X	X	X
	7 a.m.	9 a.m.	11 a.m.	1 p.m.	3 p.m.	5 p.m.	7 p.m.	9 p.m.	11 p.m.

Observations
- 7 a.m.: Kids didn't want to get ready for school; feel hot and anxious, need to keep taking time-out.
- 9 a.m.: Hot, irritable on travel to work, critical internal voice.
- 11 a.m.: Easy to chat with colleagues over tea. Able to focus on client.
- 1 p.m.: Feel sleepy after lunch, but relaxed.
- 3 p.m.: Able to focus and get tasks done, not fidgety.
- 5 p.m.: Went for after-work run, feel happy and active/alert—breathing fast and heart rate quicker but normal levels for running.
- 7 p.m.: Laughing with wife and kids playing the game, heartbeat faster and muscles a little tense/activated while competing in the game, feel happy.
- 9 p.m.: Feel relaxed and able to focus on conversation with wife.
- 11 p.m.: Feel sleepy and relaxed to sleep. Slept well.

Ursula found that after a hectic morning getting her children fed and ready for school, followed by riding her bicycle in rush hour traffic to work, her activation was high. By 11 o'clock, after her first coffee break of the day, she tended to feel much calmer. After lunch, she noticed feeling a little sleepy, but calm. The rest of the afternoon on most days she tended to feel focused and calm until the end of the workday.

However, she noticed that Tuesdays were different. She felt activated for most of the day. Upon consideration, she realized that on Tuesday mornings, in addition to the usual busy mornings, her ex-partner picked up their children from her home to take them to school. Having to interact with her ex-partner added to her increase in activation. She then saw her least stable client first thing on Tuesday mornings. Both challenges seemed to impact her ability to find a sense of calm for the rest of the day.

TUESDAY

ANS activation/ flipped lid	X	X	X						
Starting to feel ANS activation				X	X	X	X	X	X
Calm									
	7 a.m.	9 a.m.	11 a.m.	1 p.m.	3 p.m.	5 p.m.	7 p.m.	9 p.m.	11 p.m.

Observations
- 7 a.m.: Hot and fidgety, irritable, shouted at the kids for making a mess.
- 9 a.m.: Hot, irritable on travel to work, yelled at another cyclist for cutting me off on a turn.
- 11 a.m.: Client overwhelmed, kept feeling shaky myself, hard to focus.
- 1 p.m.: Not feeling hungry, tight belly and chest.
- 3 p.m.: Hard to focus, keep flitting to different tasks. Irritated by colleague's mess in the kitchen, hot feet, and chest.
- 5 p.m.: Client session went okay but felt it was hard work to stay present and look calm.
- 7 p.m.: Irritated by kids not wanting to help with chores, feel hot and muscles tense.
- 9 p.m.: Feel exhausted but jittery, irritated that I've had a hard day.
- 11 p.m.: Feel too wired to sleep, fidgety in bed; lots of thoughts running through my head. Critical voice very present.

Once she realized the pattern, Ursula took steps to change the arrangements with her ex-partner. It did not work out immediately, but did eventually. In the interim, her wife agreed that she would rearrange her Tuesday morning schedule so she could be home to send the children off to school with the ex-partner instead.

Ursula was also able to move her Tuesday morning client to Wednesday afternoon. She decided to do her administrative tasks on Tuesday mornings so that she did not see any clients the mornings she did still need to meet with her ex-partner. Continuing to track her ANS activation, she found that though Tuesday mornings continued to be a little more stressful at the moment (she was worried about how the interaction would go between her wife and ex-partner), by lunchtime after a morning of simple admin, she felt much calmer. When a difficulty arose, she noticed ANS activation, but she was able to get back to feeling calm again fairly easily.

TUESDAY

	7 a.m.	9 a.m.	11 a.m.	1 p.m.	3 p.m.	5 p.m.	7 p.m.	9 p.m.	11 p.m.
ANS activation/ flipped lid									
Starting to feel ANS activation	X	X				X			
Calm			X	X	X		X	X	X

Observations
- 7 a.m.: Heartbeat quick and feel hot and rushed before ex-partner arrives.
- 9 a.m.: Critical internal voice, heartbeat quick and breath shallow, feel hot.
- 11 a.m.: Able to focus on tasks, laughed with colleague about how we each forget the milk.
- 1 p.m.: Ate lunch with colleague, able to focus. Muscles feel relaxed.
- 3 p.m.: Easy to be present with clients.
- 5 p.m.: Disagreement with eldest child about washing up, feel hot but able to take a time-out.
- 7 p.m.: Muscles feel relaxed, easy breath and heart rate.
- 9 p.m.: Chatting with wife feels easy and comfortable, muscles relaxed.
- 11 p.m.: Feel very tired but not anxious, able to rest.

Like Ursula, it can be useful to identify when you are naturally most calm so that you can choose whether to arrange your working day around your natural rhythm.

EXERCISE Monitor Activation Throughout the Day

1. Use the tables below or draw your own in a journal to track your ANS activation. For now, this is just about tracking what is happening for you.
2. We recommend you do this over a few weeks to get a good idea. It might be useful to do continually, to keep assessing what is happening for you.
3. You could use the same tables by completing Week 1 in blue pen, Week 2 in red, Week 3 in black, and so on, noticing whether the Xs are in the same or different places those days on different weeks.
4. Remember that, like Ursula running or playing with her family, you may feel some normal activation but still be calm. This is different from feeling ANS activation. As we said earlier: Calm does not necessarily mean relaxed.

5. Once you have gathered information, notice what currently affects your ANS activation and whether anything can be changed or altered. Like Ursula, there might be some things within your current control to swap around, and you might identify things that could be changed in the future with some additional organization and support from others.

MONDAY

ANS activation/ flipped lid									
Starting to feel ANS activation									
Calm									
	7 a.m.	9 a.m.	11 a.m.	1 p.m.	3 p.m.	5 p.m.	7 p.m.	9 p.m.	11 p.m.

Observations

- _____
- _____
- _____
- _____

TUESDAY

ANS activation/ flipped lid									
Starting to feel ANS activation									
Calm									
	7 a.m.	9 a.m.	11 a.m.	1 p.m.	3 p.m.	5 p.m.	7 p.m.	9 p.m.	11 p.m.

Observations

- _____
- _____
- _____
- _____

WEDNESDAY

ANS activation/ flipped lid									
Starting to feel ANS activation									
Calm									
	7 a.m.	9 a.m.	11 a.m.	1 p.m.	3 p.m.	5 p.m.	7 p.m.	9 p.m.	11 p.m.

Observations

- _____
- _____
- _____
- _____

THURSDAY

ANS activation/ flipped lid									
Starting to feel ANS activation									
Calm									
	7 a.m.	9 a.m.	11 a.m.	1 p.m.	3 p.m.	5 p.m.	7 p.m.	9 p.m.	11 p.m.

Observations

- _____
- _____
- _____
- _____

FRIDAY

ANS activation/ flipped lid									
Starting to feel ANS activation									
Calm									
	7 a.m.	9 a.m.	11 a.m.	1 p.m.	3 p.m.	5 p.m.	7 p.m.	9 p.m.	11 p.m.

Observations

- _____
- _____
- _____
- _____

SATURDAY

ANS activation/ flipped lid									
Starting to feel ANS activation									
Calm									
	7 a.m.	9 a.m.	11 a.m.	1 p.m.	3 p.m.	5 p.m.	7 p.m.	9 p.m.	11 p.m.

Observations

- _____
- _____
- _____
- _____

SUNDAY

ANS activation/ flipped lid									
Starting to feel ANS activation									
Calm									
	7 a.m.	9 a.m.	11 a.m.	1 p.m.	3 p.m.	5 p.m.	7 p.m.	9 p.m.	11 p.m.

Observations

- _____
- _____
- _____
- _____

Monitoring ANS Using Other Factors

Your ANS level will naturally go up and down throughout the day depending on the stimulus, as shown by Ursula's experience. However, you may additionally have chronically high levels of activation, which can sometimes be affected by factors such as sleep, hunger, or mood.

EXERCISE Monitor Sleep

As described in Ursula's observations above, ANS activation can affect sleep, including difficulty getting to sleep or staying asleep, waking too early, or having bad dreams and nightmares. You may already have an idea of your current sleep patterns, but keeping track of your sleep may provide additional information or may highlight nights that are better or worse than others and point to a specific activating stimulus or useful resource.

Caveat: Be alert for a serious medical condition called *sleep apnea.** It can cause

* https://www.mayoclinic.org/diseases-conditions/sleep-apnea/symptoms-causes/syc-20377631

similar, though more extreme, symptoms but will not be relieved by stress management. If you know or you or your partner notice that you briefly stop breathing one or more times during sleep, or if you are so tired that you involuntarily fall asleep during the day, please seek a medical consultation.

1. Each morning make a note of how you slept the previous night, also jotting down any simple remarks about the previous day.

Jasper kept a log of his sleep patterns. He did not feel like he had good sleep health and often felt very tired. He attributed this to feeling so tired when he exercised and was considering reducing the amount he exercised to help with the tiredness.

However, when he looked at his sleep log, he saw that actually on the days he exercised most, he slept better. Moreover, he could see that his sleep suffered most on days he had problems at work or had more than one alcoholic drink in the evening. Below is an excerpt from his log.

	Getting to sleep	**Dreams**	**Activities in the day**
Monday	Difficult to get to sleep, ruminating about the day	No nightmares	Little exercise, lots of work on the computer; more clients than usual.
Tuesday	Fell straight asleep, but woke up in the night a couple of times	No nightmares, vivid dreams	Drank a couple of glasses of wine with friends after work.
Wednesday	Slept well	No nightmares	Work then pilates in the evening.
Thursday	Slept well	No nightmares	Work then climbing with friend.
Friday	Difficult to get to sleep	Nightmares	Work—mostly clients recovering from trauma. Watched TV after work.
Saturday	Difficult to sleep, worried about having a nightmare	No nightmares	Busy day doing household chores. Two beers with pizza.
Sunday	Difficult to sleep, thinking about client work tomorrow	No nightmares	Nice walk with partner, then got work stuff ready for the week.

2. Use the table below or a journal. Each morning when you wake up, make a note of your sleep, dreams, and brief activities of the previous day.

3. At the end of each week, review your log to notice any patterns.

4. Do this for a few weeks so that you can establish any patterns.

	Getting to sleep	Dreams	Activities in the day
Monday			
Tuesday			
Wednesday			
Thursday			
Friday			
Saturday			
Sunday			

EXERCISE   Monitor Hunger/Digestion

Similar to sleep, heightened ANS activation can affect eating habits. Adrenaline released during stress reduces hunger. However, when stress levels are chronically high, cortisol is released, which causes increased hunger, particularly for foods that offer increased energy such as those high in fat and sugar.

In this way, stress can cause weight gain or weight loss as well as digestive issues. A calm ANS state is often referred to as the "rest and digest" state, meaning that when we are in a calm state, digestion happens much more effectively. Keeping track of your hunger levels and digestion can, therefore, be a great indicator of your current stress level.

	Hunger	Digestion	Activities in the day
Example	*Didn't feel hungry at all in the morning. Hungry this evening.*	*Felt bloated after the big evening meal after not eating much all day.*	*Had a difficult meeting with highly traumatized client this morning.*
Monday			
Tuesday			
Wednesday			
Thursday			
Friday			
Saturday			
Sunday			

EXERCISE   Monitor Mood

ANS states affect moods and emotions and vice versa. A dysregulated nervous system can cause increased mood swings, depression, and irritability. As in the previous exercises, noticing when you experience these feelings can give you an indication of your nervous system state.

1. Check in with your mood every morning, midday, and evening.
2. Check the mood that best fits how you are feeling or add an alternative in an empty box.
3. Use one chart per week.
4. In the Observations area, write any influences you notice on your mood. Include common occurrences such as a particular client or an unusual occurrence such as your car breaking down.
5. When you have completed a few weeks of observation, notice if there are any signs that you are experiencing chronic ANS activation, such as often feeling a negative mood, or whether there is a regular increase in ANS activation at a certain time that may indicate an intervention might be helpful.

	Monday			Tuesday			Wednesday		
	a.m.	lunch	p.m.	a.m.	lunch	p.m.	a.m.	lunch	p.m.
Cheerful									
Happy									
Calm									
Angry									
Irritable									
Frustrated									
Sad									
Worried									
Nervous									
Afraid									
Depressed									
Sluggish									

	Thursday			Friday			Saturday			Sunday		
	a.m.	lunch	p.m.	a.m.	lunch	p.m.	a.m.	lunch	p.m.	a.m.	lunch	p.m.
Cheerful												
Happy												
Calm												
Angry												
Irritable												
Frustrated												
Sad												
Worried												
Nervous												
Afraid												
Depressed												
Sluggish												

OBSERVATIONS

Week 1: _____

_____

_____

_____

Week 2: _____

_____

_____

_____

Week 3: _____

_____

_____

_____

EXERCISE Monitor Activation Level During Client Sessions

It is particularly important to take control of your activation level during therapy sessions with your clients. Monitoring your ANS activation will make it possible for you to reduce your risk of vicarious trauma, compassion fatigue, and burnout, and it will help you to be present for your client.

In a previous exercise, you explored monitoring your general body sensations and thoughts during sessions, possibly using a timer as a reminder to check in. Adding an ANS evaluation to that check-in can be useful. It is a next step to the previous exercise and requires you both to notice what is happening for you and to additionally evaluate what that means. This will help you to learn when your activation is within a normal calm state or whether you are edging toward flipping your lid.

1. Decide upon a method for checking in with yourself during sessions. It may be using a discreet timer that a client wouldn't notice, like a gentle vibration in your pocket, or you might agree with your client that both of you will check in periodically, or you might have thought of another option best suited for you.

2. Decide on the regularity of the check-ins. For example, you might check in every 10–15 minutes in sessions with most clients and check in more frequently when you are with clients who are highly traumatized or currently exploring something that could trigger your own history.

3. Decide whether you will write down your observations or make a mental note. If you already take notes in your sessions, adding information about your own experience might be easily, and usefully, added alongside client notes. If not, you might make a table similar to the Timeline table below. You can use some of the terms or phrases from the Examples table to help you complete your timeline, or use your own.

TIMELINE					
	15 minutes	30 minutes	45 minutes	60 minutes	+15 minutes
ANS state					
Body sensations					
Quality of thoughts					
Thoughts					

Examples					
Possible body sensations	Tight chest	Soft belly	Lengthened spine	Heart beating faster	Fidgety
	Feeling stiff	Numb	Soft eyes	Sighing	Holding your breath
	Soft muscles	Cold	Heart beating steadily	Pain/aching	Sweaty
	Warm	Smiling	Frowning	Eyebrows move together	
Quality of thoughts	Racing, lots of different topics	Focus and concentrate on what I choose	Sluggish, not shifting		
Possible thoughts	I cannot do it	I love the . . .	I hate it	This reminds me of . . .	I wish it were . . .
	I do not like . . .	I am glad it is . . .	I prefer . . .	I do not understand . . .	
ANS	Calm-relaxed	Calm-active/alert	Starting to feel activated	Flipped lid	

TIME FOR AN INTERVENTION

Once you are adept at monitoring your activation level, begin to notice when you are approaching your limit. Your limit is the level beyond which you feel uncomfortable, are more at risk of compassion fatigue or vicarious traumatization, and are less able to be an effective therapist.

EXERCISE Take Stock

1. Reflect on your findings from all the exercises in the workbook up to now.
2. Have you noticed when your activation level is rising toward an uncomfortable limit in your daily life?
   a. What caused this?

   _____

   _____

   _____

   b. How did you know what your limit would be?

   _____

   _____

   _____

3. Have you noticed when your activation level is rising toward an uncomfortable limit in sessions with clients?
   a. What caused this?

   _____

   _____

   _____

   b. How did you know what your limit would be?

   _____

   _____

   _____

TAKING CONTROL OF YOUR ANS ACTIVATION LEVEL

Your Current Resources

It is likely that you already have resources for managing your ANS, or to reduce your stress level. This section of exercises will give you opportunities to take stock of the resources you already have as well as offering possible additional ones to add to your toolbox. All of our suggestions are based on what has supported therapists and other helping professionals we have worked with and what makes sense to use from a theoretical perspective. However, it is important to remember that though all resources are useful to someone, none are useful to everyone. Your toolkit should be unique to your needs and may not be like anyone else's.

What is useful can also change over time. Some resources are more or less useful in different moods, locations, and other factors. We encourage you to experiment with the resources you have found as well as the ones we share, and to continue to assess and reassess their usefulness to you.

EXERCISE Identify Your Current Resources

Make a list of resources that currently support you in regulating your nervous system and helping you to feel calm. These could be resources that you use at work, or outside of work that enable your general ability to be calm. The categories below are merely suggestions; you might prefer to organize them in another way.

Practical resources:
- *For example, regular service of car; financial stability; procedures of working to ensure safety, such as lone working policy and fire safety procedures; vacation time booked throughout the year; regularly scheduled time off each day/week.*

- _____

- _____

- _____

- _____

Social resources:

- *For example, belonging to social/community groups; supportive friend to call; peer supervision group.*

- _____
- _____
- _____
- _____
- _____
- _____

Physical resources:

- *For example, cycling; martial arts class; gardening; walking; weightlifting; yoga class; a particular yoga/qigong/movement sequence; particular breath practices or grounding practices.*

- _____
- _____
- _____
- _____
- _____
- _____

Cognitive resources:

- *For example, reading; crossword puzzles; mindfulness practices.*

- _____
- _____
- _____
- _____
- _____
- _____

Nature resources:

- *For example, gardening; communing with nature; forest bathing; walking your dog; birdwatching.*

- _____
- _____

- _____
- _____
- _____

Spiritual resources:

- _For example, religious practices; yoga; qigong; meditation; prayer._

- _____
- _____
- _____
- _____
- _____

EXERCISE   Miscellaneous Calming Resources

You may additionally have resources and practices that you already have in your toolbox that don't necessarily fit into the categories above. Note these down below.

For example, Ursula described taking a time-out, taking off a layer of clothing, wiggling her toes, and sighing a deep exhale when she felt activated.

There may be some calming resources that raise your internal critical voice, such as scrolling through social media, biting your nails, or watching old television shows. For this exercise, at least, just recognize and write any and all down without judgment.

- _____
- _____
- _____
- _____
- _____
- _____
- _____
- _____
- _____
- _____
- _____

EXERCISE Calm Your Critical Voice and Possible Alternatives

Maya was finding that she spent a lot of time on social media and that afterward she felt worse than she had before. She noticed that there were many upsetting news stories in her feed, and while staying up-to-date with current affairs was important to her, she felt that scrolling meant she wasn't in control of her intake.

She decided to be mindful to use the Favorites button so that she only scrolled through her identified close friends. She also made a photo album on her cell phone full of images that brought her a feeling of calm or joy, such as of her friends laughing, her dogs, or holidays.

When feeling a little activation, instead of scrolling through social media, where she could come across a dysregulating or triggering news story, she now scrolls through that curated album, which is a more sure-fire way to feel positive emotions.

While we have discouraged you from being self-critical of your resources, sometimes your critical voice could be hinting at something else that might be more helpful.

Reflect on the resources you identified in the previous exercise and consider whether any alternatives could be more beneficial.

Current resource	Possible alternative
_____	_____
_____	_____
_____	_____
_____	_____
_____	_____
_____	_____
_____	_____
_____	_____
_____	_____

EXERCISE Resources Reflection

1. Using different colored highlighter pens for each category, identify the resources that:
    a. Need to be done in your free time.
    b. Can be done between sessions (or immediately before or after).
    c. Can be done within sessions.
2. Reflect on the resources you have listed above. Are there any that you currently only do in your free time, that maybe you could do between sessions?
    For example, read a single page of your current book or walk around the block.

_____

_____

_____

_____

_____

_____

_____

Balance

Research has shown that physical balance is linked with emotional balance (Rajagopalan et al., 2017; Bolmont et al., 2002). Balancing uses both exteroceptive (sight and touch) and interoceptive (vestibular and proprioception) sensory information; utilizing both at the same time can potentially increase mind–body awareness. Studies have shown that PTSD affects the vestibular sense and, therefore, the capacity for physical balance. Similarly, if you experience vicarious trauma, then you may also find physical balance difficult.

Balance practice with your body or objects can offer a sense of being able to cope with uncertainty and unpredictability. It provides a way of playing with feeling wobbly and disordered and being able to stabilize yourself.

Embodied balancing can also be a great way to practice mindful body awareness. The slight risk and challenge require staying in present-moment awareness, and changing your body position to stabilize yourself gives you practice in proprioception and vestibular awareness.

You may have played games that center around the art of balancing, such as Bucka-roo, Jenga, and Twister. These can be fun ways to improve your sense of balance at the same time as connecting with friends or family.

The exercises that follow suggest ways to explore balance to facilitate your being calm and present. However, they may be useful to do when you are calm too, to add to a feeling of capacity and confidence. If you do yoga, Pilates, skiing, gymnastics, skateboarding, or martial arts and such, you may already know some exercises that improve your balancing skills. If so, explore doing some of those when you notice ANS activation so you can test whether they are useful to add to your toolbox. If you haven't already, be sure to add those balance activities to your list of resources that are useful for keeping you present, focused, and calm.

Remember that by "calm" we do not mean relaxed in your muscles. Balancing usually requires a certain amount of tension in muscles and focused attention. It may feel a little challenging. Instead, aim for calm in your ANS, so that you are not overwhelmed or have a flipped lid, and you are able to focus on the present moment with clarity and objectivity, think clearly, and make decisions. The goal is to find the optimal amount of challenge that makes it difficult enough to hold your awareness but not so difficult that you end up frustrated. The balancing exercises below are offered in steps. If you find the challenge of a particular step too great, go back to the previous step or do less. On the other hand, if you find that you are easily able to think about other things while balancing, it is likely you need to add a little more challenge.

Check in with how you feel before and after each exercise to evaluate its usefulness for you.

EXERCISE　Balance in the Palm of Your Hand

Balancing objects in your hand or on a table is one way to actively experience balance in your body if that is not appropriate or possible for you in any other way. When Vanessa was young, she found that balancing objects would help her to focus. She sometimes found it difficult to stay present at school with what the teacher was talking about and would instead find her mind wandering to something else. She discovered that a way to stay present in the classroom was to discreetly balance her pencil or pen on her finger or eraser, or to build little balancing towers of erasers and pencil sharpeners. While it took a little concentration away from what the teacher was saying, she was able to dose it so that she could focus on both at the same time.

If her mind wandered to something else, her pencil would drop, and the noise would pull her attention back to the present.

1. For this exercise you can use a pen, pencil, building block, straw, or whatever is at hand that is safe to balance on your hand.
2. Start the balancing somewhere easy, such as the palm of your hand.
3. If you would like to experiment with increased challenge to keep your focus, start to move your hand up and down, left and right, and maybe sit down and stand up as you continue to balance the object on your hand.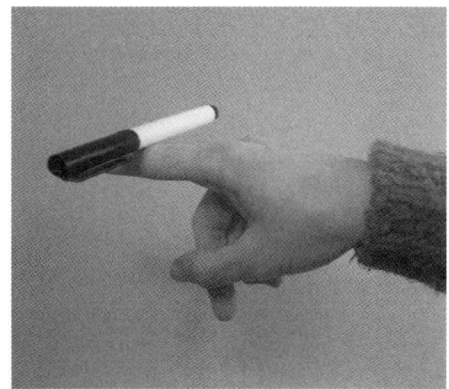
4. For the next level of challenge, experiment with looking away to the left or to the ceiling as you move the object, or even closing your eyes.
5. For an advanced challenge, experiment with balancing the object on one or two of your fingers. Then try each of the steps above with the object balancing on your finger.
6. If you find any step too challenging, return to a previous step.

EXERCISE   Balancing One Object on Another

In this exercise there is an additional factor that you need to be aware of, as well as your hand. As in the exercise above, these steps are to incrementally add challenge. Don't push to achieve every step; it is most important to identify the step that keeps your focus without too much challenge.

1. For this exercise you will need something that rolls, such as a ball or orange, and something with a flat surface, like a book.
2. Holding the flat surface, place the round object on top.
3. Move your hand around, both creating

disturbance to the round object and trying to keep it on the flat surface you are holding. Experiment with raising and lowering it, moving to the left and right.

4. Explore standing up and sitting down, moving around the room, walking, and, for more challenge, moving more quickly.

5. For greater challenge, experiment standing on one leg, then hopping, then jumping.

6. Continue to increase the challenge as you need to by experimenting with different ways to disturb the stability of the round object on the flat surface, and then righting it again.

EXERCISE Balancing Nature

Spending time outdoors has been found in many studies to increase calm and activation of the rest-and-digest state. Combining present-moment focus and embodied activities can be a potent mix. Vanessa shared an exercise similar to the one that follows in her *Wild and Well-Being Card Deck* (Bear, 2024).

1. Collect natural items with which it will be relatively easy to build a tower, such as pebbles, sticks, and tree seeds.

2. You could collect things outdoors and bring them inside or do this exercise outdoors with the potential extra challenge that weather may bring. For example, you can work out which way the wind is blowing to make things easier or more difficult.

3. On a flat surface, start to balance one of your collected objects on top of another, creating a balancing tower. It is likely to be useful to use your sense of touch to notice the flat surfaces, the uneven parts, any dimples, or protrusions to help decide which part or surface will likely be good to balance on the other.

4. Keep balancing one item on top of another. Experiment with different shapes and balances.

5. Eventually, your tower will probably fall, as in the game Jenga. Expect it so you can enjoy that as

part of the game and your balance training: identifying the point just before and just after the loss of balance.

6. If you find this easy, how could you experiment with making it more challenging?

EXERCISE Balancing an Object and Your Body

Vanessa learned this game from Elke Schroeder (personal communication, 2014), a dancer and movement teacher. Adding a playful challenge to balance objects and your body at the same time can be difficult. If you find too much challenge in this exercise, feel free to adapt it however feels right for you, skip it altogether, or come back to it at a later time.

1. You will need two children's building blocks, any other type of little block that has flat sides, or the cardboard inner of a toilet roll, or any other objects that have a flat bottom so that they can stand without falling over too easily but have an element of balance. For example, a paper cup might not be good for this, as there might be too little difficulty in it standing up, and a pencil might be too much difficulty. You will need to adapt the type of object to best suit you. If you find this too easy you might want to experiment with a pencil! If you find it too difficult, a paper cup might help!

2. Mark a spot on the floor for one foot to anchor throughout.
3. Standing on one foot, bend over and place a block on the floor in front of you, without it toppling over, then stand back up.
4. Next, balancing on one foot, bend forward and place the other block a little further away from you than the previous block. Pick up the previous block and stand back up.
5. Continue with this, placing the blocks further and further away and picking up the previously placed one. Make up the rules that best suit you. For example, you may want to change your balancing leg each time.

Strength

It may seem counterintuitive, but for many people, holding on to some tone or tension in muscles can be much more calming than muscular relaxation. A bodily sense of containment facilitated by increased muscle tone helps many people to feel held together, rather than falling apart.

With the exercises below you can explore whether strengthening and toning muscles is useful for you. It can be particularly useful for situations where you want to feel calm and present and, at the same time, have a connection to your innate strength and competency, for example, at a job interview, a session with a traumatized client, or a difficult meeting.

EXERCISE Tone Without Tension

The idea is to increase muscle tone, without becoming overly tense. This might sound contradictory, but there is a subtle difference between gripping your fingers as tightly as you can into a fist and a gentle squeeze that activates muscles but isn't exhausting or burning.

1. Gently squeeze your hand into a fist and then slowly release. Repeat.
2. Go back and forth between gentle squeeze and slow release with the aim of identifying the point at which you have muscle activation without too much exertion.
3. Take your time experimenting with this sense, using mindful awareness to help you find the right balance of tone without tension.

In the following exercises, immediately after each one, notice how it feels to maintain a little tone in the same muscles without the effort of the exercise. This may help when you would like to feel more contained.

Check in with how you feel before and after each exercise to evaluate its usefulness to you.

Each of these exercises focuses on different muscle activation so that you can explore which gives you a more calm or stable feeling. Pacing and portioning are important to the success of these exercises. The goal is to feel increased muscle tone and stability without becoming tired; a situation of "less is more."

EXERCISE   Wall Plank

1. Stand a foot or so away from a wall with your arms outstretched and palms flat on the wall. You could alternatively do this seated a foot or so away from a wall.
2. Bending your elbows, lower your chest toward the wall, keeping your feet where they are.

3. Push your chest away from the wall. The slower you push away, the more likely you will feel the muscles working in your arms and torso.
4. When you return to the start position, for a few seconds, keep a sense of the tone in your arms rather than completely releasing straightaway.
5. Notice how it feels to have a little tone in your muscles without the effort of the exercise. You may choose to maintain this small sense of muscle activation when you would like to feel contained.

EXERCISE Knee Lift

1. Get on the floor, with flat palms and knees, shins, and toes on the floor.
2. Keeping a neutral spine, with the natural curves in your spine rather than hollowed or hunched, gently lift your knees off the ground, just a couple of inches, so that you are supported by your hands and toes. You might find it more challenging to lift your knees less high, maybe an inch, so if this feels too strong, experiment with lifting higher. Or you could also start by alternately lifting just one knee at a time.
3. Keep your knees lifted long enough to mindfully notice muscle activation, but not so long that you feel fatigued.
4. Lower your knees slowly back to the ground.
5. As in the previous exercise, now that you have felt more activation in the muscles of your thighs and core, notice how it feels to continue to have a little tone in the same places, without the effort of the exercise.

EXERCISE Hand Pull

1. Sitting or standing with the natural curves in your spine, hook together the fingers of your left and right hands in front of you. Allow your shoulders and elbows to relax.
2. Keeping fingers hooked together, slowly pull your hands away from each other.
3. Notice which muscles are activated: maybe your shoulder blades, your chest, your middle back.

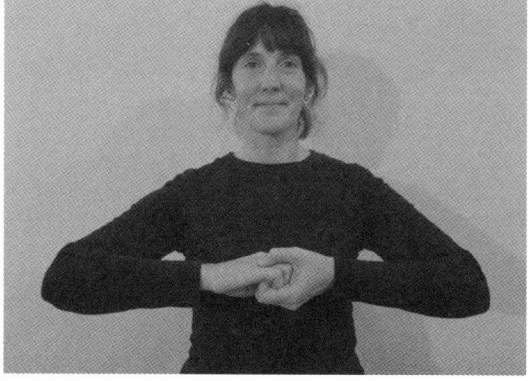

4. Slowly ease the pull until you can only minimally feel the activation in those muscles.

5. Assess how you feel.

EXERCISE Hand Push

1. Sitting or standing with the natural curves of your spine, as opposed to being hunched over, bring the palms of your hands together in front of you. Allow your shoulders and elbows to relax.

2. Push your hands against each other.

3. Notice which muscles are activated: maybe your upper arms, your abdominal muscles, your upper back.

4. Slowly soften the push until you can only minimally feel the activation in those muscles.

5. Assess how you feel.

EXERCISE Muscle Tone Reflection

In the table below, make notes of your observations of the previous strength exercises, noting which muscles or areas you noticed feeling activated. They may be different from our suggestions. Note also how you feel while doing and after doing each exercise. Indicate with a check or X whether you feel an exercise is useful for you. Blank spaces are provided for you to add additional strengthening exercises to practice.

Exercise	Muscles activated	Observations	Useful? (X or ✔)
Example **Knee lift**	Abdominal, middle back, arms, thighs	Feel powerful and capable, my body feels more held together	✔
Wall plank			
Knee lift			
Exercise	Muscles activated	Observations	Useful? (X or ✔)
Hand pull			
Hand push			

Sensory Anchors

As described in Chapter 2, memories leave somatic markers, sensations in our bodies that are linked with emotions tied to those memories. As such, somatic markers make it possible to feel sensations and emotions in the present moment from an experience (positive or negative) from our past. This phenomenon can be incredibly useful when harnessed.

When Ursula noticed that she felt more activated after seeing her ex-partner, in addition to changing her schedule she also wanted to implement other tools that would help her feel more firmly stable and calm, rather than feeling as though she could flip her lid at any time. Her supervisor asked her to make a list of her most potent memories of being calm and in control. She then asked her to take a few minutes to notice the somatic and emotional responses she had when remembering all the sensory aspects of each of those potent memories, and then identify which had the most impact on her at that moment.

Ursula identified two significant memories that, if she called on them, could possibly elicit the calm, competent, and connected responses she would like to feel on Tuesdays. The first was when she was 11 and competed at gymnastics meet. She had trained very hard but also had a lot of fun with her teammates. Although she had been a little nervous, she had mostly felt excited before her turn. Her routine went just as she had hoped, with everything going according to plan. Her body had felt strong and agile.

Following her supervisor's request, Ursula focused on remembering the final pose at the end of her routine, how she held her hands high, both feet together, her chin a little lifted. She remembered the feel of the cool blue mat under her feet and the sense of breathing hard with her heart beating fast after the exertion. The crowd had cheered and clapped, and she had seen her teammates cheering and giving her thumbs up. Her parents had stood up and waved their hands in celebration. As she recalled the memory, she noticed how right then her body mirrored her body in the memory, her spine lengthening and her chin lifting. She felt the same warmth in her chest that she had felt then, and a smile began to broaden. She felt happy and strong and connected with her powerful, competent body.

The second calming memory was when she got married to her wife. The key moment of connection and joyful calm was during the ceremony when they sang their favorite song after the vows. She recalled her wife's smiling face, the sound of their voices singing, and her friends and family all smiling. As she recalled the memory, she felt many of the same body sensations she remembered feeling then: warmth in her chest, a slight increase in heart rate, her spine lengthening, and emotions of deep joy and connectedness.

Now that she had identified these two memories, she experimented with setting aside time to think about each one, to identify which was useful and when they were useful, keeping a note of her responses. She found that thinking about the gymnastics competition helped her to feel strong and competent before meeting her ex-partner. The feeling continued after the meeting so that she felt much more grounded when going to work afterward. She also experimented with using this when she had her monthly reviews with one of her bosses whom she found quite difficult to speak to. The gymnastics memory helped her to be more able to speak confidently about her client successes as well as to be able to ask for support for the cases she found difficult without feeling deskilled or embarrassed.

Ursula noticed that the memory of her wedding ceremony was most effective in helping her regain a sense of worth, value, and connection after seeing her ex-partner. She also used it after receiving bad news or if she had received some difficult critical feedback. Connecting with the feelings of value and connected-ness helped overcome the overwhelm she sometimes experienced with criticism. Instead of flipping her lid, she was more able to respond to the feedback while maintaining self-compassion.

EXERCISE Sensory Anchors

1. Consider the situations during your week that you currently find most challenging and most likely to flip your lid. Note down the title of one of these difficult situations and the day and time it usually or most often occurs.

2. Then identify the calm that you would like to evoke, for example: competent, strong, powerful, valuable, at ease, restful, connected with others.

Situation: _____

Day: _____

Time: _____

Would like to feel: _____

Situation: _____

Day: _____

Time: _____

Would like to feel: _____

Situation: _____

Day: _____

Time: _____

Would like to feel: _____

3. Consider any memories you have of feeling the quality that you would like to feel in that situation. Note all the sensory impressions from that memory.

Memory 1, Title: _____

Saw: _____

Heard: _____

Felt: _____

Tasted: _____

Smelled: _____

Emotions: _____

Body sensations: _____

Body movements: _____

Thoughts: _____

Memory 2, Title: _____

Saw: _____

Heard: _____

Felt: _____

Tasted: _____

Smelled: _____

Emotions: _____

Body sensations: _____

Body movements: _____

Thoughts: _____

Memory 3, Title: _____

Saw: _____

Heard: _____

Felt: _____

Tasted: _____

Smelled: _____

Emotions: _____

Body sensations: _____

Body movements: _____

Thoughts: _____

4. Check in with how you are feeling right now, then notice what changes as you do this step. Recall each memory, one at a time, and make a note of your responses to the memory in the present moment.

Memory 1, Present-moment response:

Emotions: _____

Body sensations: _____

Body movements: _____

Thoughts: _____

Memory 2, Present-moment response:

Emotions: _____

Body sensations: _____

Body movements: _____

Thoughts: _____

Memory 3, Present-moment response:

Emotions: _____

Body sensations: _____

Body movements: _____

Thoughts: _____

5. Based on what you have noticed, consider when it would be most useful to consciously recall each of the memories you have identified. Like Ursula, maybe one would be more useful before a challenging situation, or afterward, or possibly during. It is likely that noticing how you might feel and how you would like to feel for each scenario will help you to decide.

Situation 1:

Memory title: _____

Day: _____

Time: _____

Feeling intended to evoke: _____

Emotions: _____

Body sensations: _____

Body movements: _____

Thoughts: _____

Outcome: Useful / No effect / Negative effect

Situation 2:

Memory title: _____

Day: _____

Time: _____

Feeling intended to evoke: _____

Emotions: _____

Body sensations: _____

Body movements: _____

Thoughts: _____

Outcome: Useful / No effect / Negative effect

Situation 3:

Memory title: _____

Day: _____

Time: _____

Feeling intended to evoke: _____

Emotions: _____

Body sensations: _____

Body movements: _____

Thoughts: _____

Outcome: Useful / No effect / Negative effect

EXERCISE Remembering the Movements of Sensory Anchors

Like Ursula, you may notice your muscles and body movement mirror what you are recalling. Doing this consciously can be a useful addition to evoking the past feelings of the memory. Just as thinking about something can evoke bodily responses, so can bodily expression create responses in your mind.

1. Choose a memory where you felt calm. It could be one you identified in the previous exercise or something different.
2. Recall the physical stance or movement you had in that memory. For Ursula, it would be at the end of her gymnastic performance, standing with her arms aloft, feet together and chin lifted.
3. Write a description or draw it here:

4. Next, actually assume that stance or movement, moving your own body in the present into the same posture as the memory from the past. Stay in the position or movement for as long as it feels useful, perhaps a couple of minutes; set a timer if that would be helpful

5. Make a note of your response.

6. If the response was positive, consider when it would be useful to use this resource.

7. You could also think of a more subtle adaptation that you could do when the full posture or movement isn't possible. For example, Ursula could not raise her arms in a meeting with colleagues, her boss, or a client, but she could easily put her feet together and lengthen her spine, and even raise her chin a little without causing any distraction.

8. Consider keeping your drawing or description somewhere that you will see it as a reminder to do it when you need to reconnect with that feeling.

Feeling intended to evoke: _____

Memory: _____

Description or drawing of body in the memory:

Outcome: Useful / No effect / Negative effect

Emotions: _____

Body sensations: _____

Body movements: _____

Thoughts: _____

Subtle adaptation: _____

_____

When to use it: _____

_____

SENSORY ANCHORS IN NATURE

Vanessa works as an eco-psychotherapist with adults and children outdoors and often notices that people use the metaphor of what they see, hear, smell, and feel in nature to describe their emotions. Her *Wild and Well-Being Card Deck* includes an exercise similar to the previous one, though rather than using a personal memory to evoke a quality or feeling, she introduces the idea of noticing a quality in nature instead (Bear, 2024). This was the basis of the exercise in Chapter 2, "Explore Mirroring in Nature."

Vanessa came to that idea after she experimented with purposefully exploring how she was affected by noticing things in nature that expressed how she would like to feel. Wanting to feel strong and stable, she found a huge oak tree. Initially, she noticed everything about it, how the tree's trunk was solid and broad, its roots spread out and going deep into the ground around it, and how its branches were held aloft and wide.

Next, she copied the posture of the oak tree with her own body, rooting her feet into the ground, making her torso broad and upright, lifting her spine as if moving toward the sun. She raised her arms aloft like branches. At first, she felt a little silly, and her muscles felt tense, but as she saw the branches moving in the wind, she softened her own shoulders and felt more at ease. She was surprised at how quickly she felt a sense of solidity and strength and her body, mind, and emotions felt connected.

She took a photograph of the tree and pinned a copy in her office as a reminder to embody it whenever she wanted to evoke those feelings again.

The first part of this exercise aims to evoke the qualities of a mountain. It was originally published in the *Wild and Well-Being Card Deck* (Bear, 2024). In the second part, like Vanessa, you will have the opportunity to consciously look for the qualities you would like to feel.

EXERCISE Connect With the Qualities of Mountains

Observing qualities in the external environment can help you identify the same qualities in yourself, or the potential for them. Recognizing these qualities will also help you to remember that you are not separate from nature—we are all nature, and we all belong.

1. You can do this exercise either in a place with a mountain view, looking at a photograph of a mountain, or recalling a memory of a mountain.
2. Watch, imagine, or remember any clouds and weather moving around the mountain. Pay attention to the mountain's steadiness and solidity.
3. What signs of life you can see (or remember) around the mountain: trees, plants, animals, insects, and so on.
4. Identify contours, shapes, light, and shadows in what you are seeing or remembering.
5. Distinguish the evident and subtle activity around the mountain from the mountain's steadiness and stillness.
6. Standing or sitting with an upright spine, adjust your posture to mirror the mountain's quiet steadiness.
7. Notice if parts of your body are steady and still right now. Pay attention to larger and smaller body parts, all the way to the tips of your toes and fingers.

EXERCISE Mirror Nature

1. Look for or remember animals and plants that seem to represent a feeling or emotion for you that you would like to cultivate.
2. Explore mimicking the movement or stance you see or remember, for example spreading your "wings" as a bird or curling into a ball like a furled fern, standing tall with ears pricked like a horse who has heard a sound, and so on.
3. Notice what this evokes in you.
4. If it was pleasant or calming, when might it be useful to evoke that feeling?
5. How will you remember to evoke it? Maybe take a photograph, draw it, or write a description.

Experiment 1

Nature mirrored: _____

Intended quality: _____

Emotion: _____

Body sensations: _____

Thoughts: _____
Positive response / Neutral / Negative response

When I will use it: _____

_____

How I will remember: photograph / drawing / written description / other

_____

Experiment 2

Nature mirrored: _____

Intended quality: _____

Emotion: _____

Body sensations: _____

Thoughts: _____
Positive response / Neutral / Negative response

When I will use it: _____

_____

How I will remember: photograph / drawing / written description / other

_____

Experiment 3

Nature mirrored: _____

Intended quality: _____

Emotion: _____

Body sensations: _____

Thoughts: _____
Positive response / Neutral / Negative response

When I will use it: _____

_____

How I will remember: photograph / drawing / written description / other

_____

YOUR COMFORT ZONE AND BOUNDARIES

On the first day of Ursula's new job, one of her new colleagues approached to welcome her. As the colleague approached, rather than stopping at a distance that Ursula would have found comfortable (and appropriate), the colleague continued to walk closer and closer toward her. Ursula suddenly felt a little panic, her heart rate increased, and she noticed she was holding her breath. Though she wanted to take a step backward, she felt sort of stuck and was unable to understand what was being said. Only once the colleague had left the room did Ursula sigh a long exhale. She realized that the colleague moving so quickly and into her personal space had caused her to momentarily flip her lid.

Ursula recalled a similar experience when she went for therapy a few years before. The therapy room had been quite large, but the therapist and client chairs were set up very close together and directly in front of each other; there was no table or space between them. She had felt very uncomfortable sitting so close to the therapist but was afraid it might be rude to push her chair back.

When Ursula moved to another town, she found a different therapist. In the first few sessions, the new therapist invited Ursula to experiment with where she sat in the room, which had a few chairs in different places: one facing the door, one near a window, and one that would put a large desk between her and the therapist. She found that when she sat in the chair with the desk in front of her, she felt much calmer, her shoulders dropped, and she could breathe much easier. It was as though the desk offered a comfortable boundary between her and the new therapist.

Ursula took this experience into her own practice and offered similar distance and seating options to her clients. However, several of them chose seats very close

to her with nothing between them. As the therapist, she did not feel it was okay for her to refuse them, or to share her personal response to them being so close. She did not want her discomfort to affect the therapeutic relationship or for the client to feel shamed by her response. However, she noticed that with those clients, she felt significantly less grounded and stable, and it was much easier to get caught up in their distress.

Ursula's supervisor was not at all surprised that it was more difficult for her to separate herself from her client's distress when sitting too close. The supervisor disagreed with Ursula's view that she must meet the client's needs at the expense of her own. She reminded Ursula that her clients deserved to have a grounded, present therapist who had their lid firmly in place. The supervisor suggested Ursula could continue to offer her clients choice while also ensuring Ursula had the boundary of a desk or table. She suggested that Ursula place her chair behind a table. Then she could stipulate that clients experiment with moving their chair to different angles and distances from the table. This would ensure that Ursula had a physical boundary, and the clients could experiment with their needs too.

Knowing your physical comfort zone with other people can be incredibly important in being able to connect with a sense of calm and grounded presence. Like Ursula, you might already know that having a table or desk as a physical boundary helps you. It might be that you don't have space for a table or desk, but a clipboard on your lap for your notes could offer boundary enough. You might prefer facing the door or being the closest to the door so that you can exit easily if you need to. You might find it more calming to face a window, to have natural light, or you may find that too distracting. Knowing what your preferences and responses are can be integral in ensuring you feel present and calm in your professional space.

You may be concerned that increasing physical distance and creating a boundary makes it harder to connect with your client. However, as Ursula's supervisor advised, it can actually increase your ability to be useful. Within your own secure personal space, you can be compassionate instead of empathetic (see Chapter 2). You will actually be more useful to your client when you are not getting caught up in their whirlpool.

Note that boundaries change all the time, even in the same room and with the same person. So do not consider the results of the exercises below to be valid for all time. Instead, let the exercises help you get accustomed to frequently evaluating the comfort of your physical space and adjusting accordingly.

EXERCISE   Assess Your Physical Boundaries

In this exercise you will need a partner, maybe a friend or family member, or a colleague, so that you can both experiment with what is right for you. You may already have a sense of where your personal space limits are. Like Ursula with her colleague, you might have a strong reaction when your space is intruded upon. If you choose to do this exercise, make sure to take the steps slowly. Remember that anyone participating in an exercise can pause it at any time, take a time-out, or opt-out altogether. As this exercise involves experimenting with physical space and ANS activation, make sure you choose a person that you trust and generally feel comfortable and safe with. Likewise, they should feel comfortable with you and able to honestly share their own responses.

1. Decide who is Person A and Person B. Go through these steps and then swap.
2. Agree on how you will communicate to guide your partner forward, backward, left, right, and stop. This can be words, hand signals, or whatever communication mode you agree on.
3. Person A stands at one end of a room.
4. Person A directs Person B forward and backward (not left and right for now). Simply instruct them to move toward and away from you. Do this slowly, one direction at a time, while continually checking in with your body sensations, mood, and thoughts.
5. Whenever Person A notices a change in their own body sensation, mood, or thought response, say or give the agreed stop sign. Note where Person B is standing when this occurs. Person A evaluates if this is a positive response or a negative response and if it indicates that Person B is too close or too far away.
6. Person A continues to experiment, identifying the spot where Person B becomes too close and the spot where Person B feels too far away. You can also experiment to discover if it is useful or not to maintain eye contact during this exercise, and if that gives more information.
7. Next, establish a distance where Person A feels the most comfortable.
8. Person A reports on how they know they feel comfortable, what changes in their response that equates to comfort.
9. Once Person A has identified the most comfortable distance forward and backward, experiment in the same way with left and right. Person A directs Person

B left and right to find the comfort spot. Person A reports how they know that it is right for them. Pause for a few moments with the current distance. Check in with what that feels like. Person A writes down what happens in their body, mood, and thoughts when the distance is optimal for them. This way they will be more able to recognize that sense again.

10. Swap roles and repeat.

EXERCISE Identify Your Chair

If you work regularly in the same location, you can do this exercise and then keep your office set up in the best way for you. If you usually work in different places or rooms, it will give you an idea of the positioning that you would likely find most calming so that you can arrange chairs and furniture before each session to best suit your preferences.

1. Experiment with moving your chair into the suggested positions as well as any others you can think of appropriate to the room and clientele where you work.
2. As you sit in each place, notice your body sensations, posture, mood, and thoughts, and write your observations below.
3. Assess the place in the room you feel most comfortable, considering and possibly combining each of the suggestions. For example, the calmest response might be to sit behind a desk, near the door, angled to the right.
4. Test out your findings by inviting a friend or colleague to move their chair into different places around the room, while you remain in the spot you identified as most comfortable. As they move their chair, continue to monitor your response. If you do note a negative response, explore what could be changed about your position for you to feel calm again; maybe angling your chair in a different direction or some such.

Location of therapist chair	Body sensation and posture response	Mood response	Thought/cognitive response
Near a window			
Opposite a window			
Near a door			
Opposite a door			
Behind a desk			
Behind a table			
Angled straight opposite client chair			
Angled left of client chair			
Angled right of client chair			

EXERCISE   Consider the Alternatives

> *When Ursula worked in the health service during the height of COVID-19, she was often moved to other rooms due to the increased need for distanced working and different parts of the medical center being used for vaccinations.*
>
> *Ursula had realized that working without a table in between her and clients made her feel less calm, but many of the offices she was allocated to did not have a table or desk. Ursula experimented with bringing in a little fold-up table. This increased her sense of a boundary and offered a more aesthetically pleasing feel to the otherwise quite clinical rooms.*

If you do not work in the same room every day, or if you work within an organization where your location changes regularly, it may be useful to consider alternatives depending on what you have noticed in the previous exercise.

1. Consider your preferences from the exercise above.
2. What would offer an alternative to your preferences?
3. Make a list to experiment with, noticing your response to assess which is most effective.

Preferred location of therapist chair	Alternative (e.g., clipboard instead of a table; a photograph of nature scene in place of a window)	Body sensation and posture response; mood response; thought/cognitive response
Near a window		
Opposite a window		
Near a door		
Opposite a door		

Preferred location of therapist chair	Alternative (e.g., clipboard instead of a table; a photograph of nature scene in place of a window)	Body sensation and posture response; mood response; thought/cognitive response
Behind a desk		
Behind a table		
Angled straight opposite client chair		
Angled left of client chair		
Angled right of client chair		

EXERCISE Give Yourself Space (Face-to-Face)

In addition to finding the right spot for your chair, it can be useful to rearrange your office to give yourself as many options as possible for moving closer and further away. For example, if you feel most comfortable behind a desk, you may choose to have the desk away from a wall, giving you the option to move backward and forward, to the left and to the right.

1. Using the space below, draw your office, approximately to scale.
2. On a separate piece of paper, draw the items of furniture approximately to scale and cut each of them out so that you can play with the layout of furniture in the room.
3. Experiment with different layouts that you feel would be most calming for you and offer the most flexibility for you to move around to create distance if you need it.
4. Once you have worked it out on paper, try the arrangement in your office to match and test out whether it works, checking in with your ANS to notice if you feel more calm or more activated.

EXERCISE   Give Yourself Space (Online)

Despite being physically far removed from one another, exploring distance when working online is just as important. When in person, a therapist would be very unlikely to sit so close to someone that they can see their individual eyebrow hairs, and yet many people sit that close to their computer screen and webcam. This habit can unconsciously cause a feeling of being overexposed or a sense of being much too close for your nervous system (and possibly also your client's).

1. Arrange an online meeting with a colleague or friend who has agreed to help you with this exercise.
2. Similarly to the previous exercise, track your body sensations, mood, and thoughts, as you move in relation to your computer screen.
3. First, try moving your body back and forward, closer to and further from the screen; sometimes just sitting back in your chair can make a big difference.
4. Next, move your chair backward and forward in front of the screen. You can try each while either looking away or continuing to maintain contact with the person on-screen.
5. Once you find the spot for your chair where you feel most calm, mark it on the floor or carpet so that you can be sure to easily find it again.
6. Explore moving left and right to see where is the calmest for you on that plane too.
7. During client sessions, start from the place you have marked on the floor. Pay attention with various clients if there is a difference in your impulses to move in this direction or that. Take note of your preferred spot for each client so that you can start their session from that spot, even if you then change in a small or bigger way. Continue to assess.

Boundaries in the Therapy Room

In addition to physical distance, there are other ways to create a sense of space or a boundary between you and a client. It may be important to ensure that you are easily able to avoid being affected by their ANS activation. That will make it possible for you to remain calm and present, and therefore as useful, as possible.

EXERCISE Keeping Calm Using Eye Contact

Studies have shown that eye contact increases empathy; in order to mirror someone, you need to be able to see them. As described in Chapter 2, being able to moderate and be in control of the amount of empathy you feel, while maintaining compassion, can be essential. It will allow you to be separate enough from your clients to be able self-regulate.

The importance of maintaining eye contact will vary among your clients. Some will feel it important for feeling a connection with you. On the other hand, there are also many who may find constant eye contact intrusive, overbearing, shaming, or even triggering. This might also be something you decide to talk about with your individual clients, experimenting with what is right for them individually.

In this workbook though, the focus is you. While client needs are important, so are yours, as they affect not only your well-being but also your effectiveness with your clients. Experimenting will be useful for both of you. In fact, most clients will not want or be comfortable with constant eye contact. And some clients will discover that their sense of contact with you actually increases when it is possible to periodically break eye contact. Daniel Stern (1985) describes how infants and mothers found that bonding was stronger when the baby was allowed to periodically break eye contact with the mother. He found this allowed the baby to learn to self-regulate its nervous system by taking breaks from the excitation of contact. This periodic looking away facilitated gradually building greater contact tolerance.

1. Partner with a colleague or friend and set a timer for 2 minutes.
2. Have a pen or pencil and a piece of paper available.
3. Ask your partner to talk about an agreed conversational (*not* traumatic) topic for the 2 minutes.
4. Maintain eye contact the entire 2 minutes.
5. Notice how that feels, and write down any observations.
6. Again, ask your partner to talk about an agreed topic for 2 minutes.
7. Each time you naturally feel a desire to break eye contact, do so, and mark your paper.
8. Notice how you feel when you break eye contact and when you return to it.
9. Notice how you feel during and after the conversation.
10. Next, do the same again, with your partner speaking for 2 minutes, but this time

consciously look away now and then into the distance, maybe out the window or to the side. It only needs to be for a couple of seconds.

11. Notice how you feel when you break eye contact and when you return to it.

12. If you are worried about seeming distracted, you can use nonverbal listening cues, such as nodding your head as you look away to show you are still with them.

13. Notice how you feel during and after these conversations. Ask your partner about their experience too.

14. Experiment with periodic looking away while talking with clients. Keep a log of how it feels to be able to look away from them from time to time. Is it the same or different with various clients?

15. Make a plan for how you will remember to take a break from eye contact now and then.

EXERCISE Eye Boundary

Similarly to the muscle-toning exercises, holding some light muscle tone around your eyes can sometimes create a sense of distance and boundary.

Practice first in a mirror, as it can feel as though it is much less subtle than it looks. You can also practice with a friend or colleague and get their feedback before using it with a client so that you will feel confident that you are not giving them menacing looks!

1. Notice the muscles around your eyes. It may help to first really tense them up and then gradually release the tension completely to compare completely soft eyes with completely tense eyes. For those of you who do not know what "soft" or "tense" eyes feel like, or cannot distinguish the difference, try having the sense of pushing someone or something away with your eyes (tense) and inviting someone or something closer with your eyes (soft). Another way is to unfocus your eyes (soft) and then make your focus as sharp as possible (tense).

2. Move between tensing and softening a few times, noticing how your muscles change for each.

3. Hold the tension around your eyes for around 30 seconds and notice any response.

Body sensation: _____

Mood: _____

Thoughts: _____

Other: _____

4. Completely soften the tension around your eyes for around 30 seconds and notice any response.

Body sensation: _____

Mood: _____

Thoughts: _____

Other: _____

5. Next, experiment with moving in between these two, finding the right amount of tension that has a sense of boundary (pushing away).

   If you are comfortable doing so, use a mirror to continue to experiment, noticing how this amount of tension looks. Notice your response:

Body sensation: _____

Mood: _____

Thoughts: _____

Other: _____

6. Experiment with the amount of tension or tone around your eyes that feels useful as a boundary, without you worrying that it looks too noticeable. Note, however, it will be very few people who will actually notice a change in the tension around your eyes.

7. Next, with a partner, alternate increasing and decreasing the eye tensing during a 2-minute conversation. Your partner can do the same or not depending on what you two agree on. Discuss with your partner afterward what each of you noticed.

Body sensation: _____

Mood: _____

Thoughts: _____

Other: _____

| EXERCISE | Clothing Boundaries |

Merriam-Webster's dictionary (2024) describes the idiom "thick skin" to mean "an ability to keep from getting upset or offended by the things other people say and do." As such, a sense of a literally thick skin can be useful to keep calm and feel separation from your client. This exercise explores using clothing as a way to "thicken your skin."

Ursula had a particular client who would come into the room in a shaking rage with the world. No matter how much Ursula tried to keep her empathy dial on low, to stay steady and calm, she nonetheless felt exposed and vulnerable to being strongly affected by the client's ANS activation.

She spoke with her supervisor, and they discussed how she might change the room so that she had more of a boundary, perhaps using her desk, and then discussed possible countertransference.

It turned out that Ursula's room layout was not the issue; in fact she felt bolstered by it. In addition, the client's issues were very different from her own. Since it appeared neither of those were making Ursula more vulnerable, her supervisor tried a different tactic and asked Ursula what she tended to wear to work.

Ursula described the beautiful dresses, kurtas, tunics, and shawls that she usually wore. While it sounded like Ursula looked fabulous, the materials of most of her clothes were very thin and floaty. Her supervisor wondered if Ursula would be willing to keep track of what she wore and how she felt with the client, suggesting that one session she try wearing her usual clothes and one session wearing something much thicker and sturdier.

They discussed some options. Ursula felt the greatest sensation of vulnerability at her chest and decided on a long cardigan that would fully cover her chest and was still in her usual style but was made from thicker fabric. Ursula also described a brooch that had belonged to her feisty great-grandmother, a matriarch of the family. She decided to add another test, wearing that brooch as a protective medallion that might also help her to connect with the qualities she shared with her great-grandmother.

A few weeks later, Ursula reported her findings. She had realized that a particular tunic she regularly wore in her work rotation was actually connected to a very sad family event. She hadn't even considered it before, but by paying more attention, she realized that whenever she wore that tunic, she felt much more easily affected by all of her clients. She decided that she would not wear that to work anymore.

Ursula described a marked difference wearing the thicker cardigan. She had felt stronger and the tight feelings of exposure in her chest, had gone. Instead, she felt more able to connect to her own capability and remain calm through the session. The brooch had enabled her to create a ritual before the session. When pinning it on, she had recalled the image of her great-grandmother and felt her body mirror that image she had in her mind. She instantly felt more capable and more in her own skin. Ursula decided that she would use the same test with each of her clients, working out which ones she felt she needed an extra sense of boundary with. With some clients, wearing the brooch was enough. With others, she put on her thick cardigan, which she now kept on the back of her chair, in case she unexpectedly needed it with a client.

1. In the table below, make a note of what you wear to work each day for a week. Add the initials of the clients you see and mark down your self-observations from the sessions.
2. Using a highlighter pen or placing a star, notice which clients provoked the most ANS activation for you.
3. Notice any areas of your body that feel particularly vulnerable.

_____

_____

_____

_____

_____

_____

Monday

Client's initials	What you wore	Observations of your body sensations, mood, thoughts in the session
	Week 1:	
	Week 2:	
	Week 3:	
	Week 1:	
	Week 2:	
	Week 3:	
	Week 1:	
	Week 2:	
	Week 3:	
	Week 1:	
	Week 2:	
	Week 3:	

Tuesday

Client's initials	What you wore	Observations of your body sensations, mood, thoughts in the session
	Week 1:	
	Week 2:	
	Week 3:	
	Week 1:	
	Week 2:	
	Week 3:	
	Week 1:	
	Week 2:	
	Week 3:	
	Week 1:	
	Week 2:	
	Week 3:	

Wednesday

Client's initials	What you wore	Observations of your body sensations, mood, thoughts in the session
	Week 1:	
	Week 2:	
	Week 3:	
	Week 1:	
	Week 2:	
	Week 3:	
	Week 1:	
	Week 2:	
	Week 3:	
	Week 1:	
	Week 2:	
	Week 3:	

Thursday

Client's initials	What you wore	Observations of your body sensations, mood, thoughts in the session
	Week 1:	
	Week 2:	
	Week 3:	
	Week 1:	
	Week 2:	
	Week 3:	
	Week 1:	
	Week 2:	
	Week 3:	
	Week 1:	
	Week 2:	
	Week 3:	

Friday

Client's initials	What you wore	Observations of your body sensations, mood, thoughts in the session
	Week 1:	
	Week 2:	
	Week 3:	
	Week 1:	
	Week 2:	
	Week 3:	
	Week 1:	
	Week 2:	
	Week 3:	
	Week 1:	
	Week 2:	
	Week 3:	

4. Consider whether you were wearing any of the same items of clothing when you had a recurring pattern of activation. Consider if that may have a connection with vulnerability or difficulty, as with Ursula's tunic. Make a note of which items they are and decide when you will and will not wear them, or whether it would be better not to wear them to work at all.

   Items of clothing that are connected with difficulty:

   _____

   _____

   _____

5. Consider items of clothing in your closet that would be comfortable and offer you a sense of thicker skin, particularly in those areas of your body that feel most vulnerable. For Ursula it made sense to cover her vulnerable chest with a thick cardigan. For you it may be wearing denim trousers, rather than a skirt, over vulnerable-feeling legs, or thick leggings or tights under a skirt; another idea might be wearing clear prescription-free glasses (if you don't need them) over vulnerable eyes.

6. Observe how you feel wearing each item with your clients, noting whether it is useful, no change, or not useful. You may need to experiment a few times to give a fair trial.

   Clothing: _____

   Days and times to wear it: _____
   Observations of its effect:
   - ☐ Felt better
   - ☐ Felt worse
   - ☐ No effect

   Other observations: _____

   _____

   Clothing: _____

   Days and times to wear it: _____
   Observations of its effect:
   - ☐ Felt better
   - ☐ Felt worse
   - ☐ No effect

Other observations: _____

_____

7. Also consider any items that bring you a sense of being strengthened, such as Ursula's great-grandmother's brooch or Wonder Woman's bracelets. It could be an heirloom or something with a symbol that has a powerful message to you, such as a tree: strong, rooted, flexible in the wind.

Object: _____

Message / symbolism: _____

Days and times to wear it: _____

Observations of its effect:

☐ Felt better

☐ Felt worse

☐ No effect

Other observations: _____

_____

Object: _____

Message / symbolism: _____

Days and times to wear it: _____

Observations of its effect:

☐ Felt better

☐ Felt worse

☐ No effect

Other observations: _____

_____

8. If you find that the item is useful, decide where you will keep it so that it is at hand before the sessions with clients who might provoke an unhelpful reaction in you. It may be easier to choose something that you can wear all day (like a necklace pendant) or something that would be easy to put on during a session (for example, it would not seem unusual to put on a cardigan during a session).

REFLECTIONS ON KEEPING CALM

The exercises in this chapter have focused on deepening your self-awareness of calm versus ANS activation and tools for you to use to stay calm or to help you maintain or get your lid back on. Some will hopefully be useful for you, while others will be less useful or not useful altogether or at particular times or in particular situations.

The following exercise is meant to help you to take stock of what has and has not been useful in this chapter. It will enable you to have an at-a-glance guide that you can refer to when planning your weekly schedule, including chosen exercises at the times when you anticipate them being most useful. Continue to assess their effectiveness and update your table regularly as the experiences of using them give you more information.

Ursula decided that every Friday afternoon she would reflect on the week before and highlight when she had experienced ANS activation, which of the resources had been useful and which had not been effective. She took some time to reflect on those that had not been effective and consider if she should just drop them or whether she could alter them in any way or try them at an alternative time.

Then she would look at the schedule for the following week and highlight any client sessions, meetings, or events that she anticipated might cause ANS activation. She considered each of the resources she had identified as useful and applied the information gathered about the previous week to inform her future choices. She marked each of these directly into her diary so that she would remember to do them and made a firm decision to take these self-care appointments as seriously as the appointments with clients and others.

EXERCISE Calm Resources Inventory

1. Make a comprehensive list of resources that help you to keep calm, remembering that calm means not having a flipped lid and being able to think clearly, rather than being relaxed in your muscles. Include all the resources you added in the Identify Your Current Resources exercise as well as the others you found in this workbook or learned elsewhere.

2. Assess the current usefulness of each, giving a score. Do not worry if you are not yet able to do this; you may need to experiment more with one or more resource first, particularly resources you haven't used for a while or are completely new to you.

3. Estimate when you think a resource would be useful. For example, it might be that you decide to do wall planks before each session, or a walk in nature each morning to find a tree to mirror, or you may choose to balance objects between each client you see. You might assess at the beginning of each workday whether the room layout is good for you that day or whether anything needs changing. For example, on a hot day you might prefer to have a fan in the room and decide where to place it.

4. Continue to evaluate and experiment with your resources, remembering that every resource will be good for some people, but none are good for everyone. Moreover, any resource's value to you can shift and might be good one day and not the next or vice versa. Notice if you are self-critical because a resource doesn't work as well as you'd hoped. Instead, assess and experiment with something different. Notice any patterns so that you can get more skilled at predicting what will be most useful for you and when it will be most useful.

Resource (put your resources from your current resources in the blank boxes)	Usefulness (–10 = abreaction; 0 = neutral; 10 = extremely useful)	Type of calm (e.g., relaxed / strong / capable/ empowered / present / focused)	When it is likely to be most useful (e.g., before work/ after work / between clients / at the end of the day)
Self check-in			
Mindful eating			
Mindful shifting			
Check-in reminders			

Resource (put your resources from your current resources in the blank boxes)	Usefulness (−10 = abreaction; 0 = neutral; 10 = extremely useful)	Type of calm (e.g., relaxed / strong / capable/ empowered / present / focused)	When it is likely to be most useful (e.g., before work/ after work / between clients / at the end of the day)
Calm your critical voice			
Balance in the palm of your hand			
Balancing one object on top of another			
Balancing nature			
Balancing an object and your body			
Wall plank			
Knee lift			
Hand pull			
Hand push			
Sensory anchor			

Resource (put your resources from your current resources in the blank boxes)	Usefulness (−10 = abreaction; 0 = neutral; 10 = extremely useful)	Type of calm (e.g., relaxed / strong / capable/ empowered / present / focused)	When it is likely to be most useful (e.g., before work/ after work / between clients / at the end of the day)
Remembering the movements of sensory anchors			
Connect with the qualities of mountains			
Mirror nature			
Identify your chair			
Give yourself space			
Eye contact			
Eye boundary			
Clothing boundaries			

Resource (put your resources from your current resources in the blank boxes)	Usefulness (−10 = abreaction; 0 = neutral; 10 = extremely useful)	Type of calm (e.g., relaxed / strong / capable/ empowered / present / focused)	When it is likely to be most useful (e.g., before work/ after work / between clients / at the end of the day)

EXERCISE   Calm Resources Plan

1. Decide on a day each week when you will assess your appointment calendar, noting when you expect to have more susceptibility to ANS activation. Mark this time in your calendar or diary now. If you have an electronic calendar, decide if you want to set the appointment to automatically repeat and to send you a reminder.

2. On your decided assessment day, look back over the past week and make a note of the events that caused ANS activation.

3. Make note of which resources were useful and which were not.

4. Consider any adjustments or adaptations to the resources and whether you will experiment with something different next week.

5. Assess your diary for the coming week. Highlight any appointments, personal or work related, that may cause activation.

6. Using your inventory from the previous exercise, choose resources to use for each of these events, deciding whether you will use the resource before, during, or afterward. Mark the resource in your diary accordingly, just like any other important appointment.

   - Difficult situation from previous week:

     _____

     _____

     Resource used: _____
     Used: Before / During / After
     Outcome: Useful / No effect / Negative effect

     Future adaptation: _____

   - Difficult situation from previous week:

     _____

     _____

     Resource used: _____
     Used: Before / During / After
     Outcome: Useful / No effect / Negative effect

     Future adaptation: _____

• Difficult situation from previous week:

_____

_____

Resource used: _____

Used: Before / During / After

Outcome: Useful / No effect / Negative effect

Future adaptation: _____

CHAPTER 4

Thinking Clearly

Thinking clearly is essential to making good decisions in life, and for our purposes here, both about your self-care and about your work. Stress and autonomic nervous system (ANS) dysregulation make thinking clearly more difficult. This chapter contains exercises to explore ways to reduce stress and maintain clear thinking.

KEEPING YOUR BRAIN CALM

A useful model to explain the link between keeping calm and thinking clearly is Paul MacLean's (1985) concept of the Triune Brain which parallels the three key areas of the brain, which were also discussed in Chapter 3 in the section on the Illustrating the Brain à la Dan Siegel. Below is a brief review:

1. Reptilian: This part of the brain is responsible for the mostly unconscious systems of our bodies that are essential for us to stay alive, such as heart rate and balance.

   It consists of the brain stem and cerebellum.

   You can also think of this reptilian part as your survival brain.

   Communicates with: sensations

2. Limbic system: This part of the brain is responsible for emotions, attachment, and survival responses, including fight-or-flight response, sending and receiving hormones, and processing memories.

   It consists of the thalamus, hypothalamus, amygdala, and hippocampus.

   You can also think of the limbic system as your emotional brain.

   Communicates with: feelings

3. Neocortex: This part of the brain is the most recently evolved and makes it possible for humans to plan, judge, and have rational thought and voluntary movement.

You can also think of the neocortex as your thinking brain.

Communicates with: words

In Chapter 3, we referred to Dan Siegel's Hand Model of the Brain. The Triune Brain Model would map onto that model with the reflective learning or thinking brain (neocortex) as the fingers of the hand, the emotional learning brain (amgydala and hypothalamus) as the thumb, and the survival brain (brain stem and cerebellum) as the palm of the hand.

How the different parts of our brain communicate with each other and with other parts of the body is key to understanding the difference between clear thinking and not clear thinking. When the sensory nervous system takes information from the external environment, in simple terms, it is processed in two ways—fast and slow (see image below).

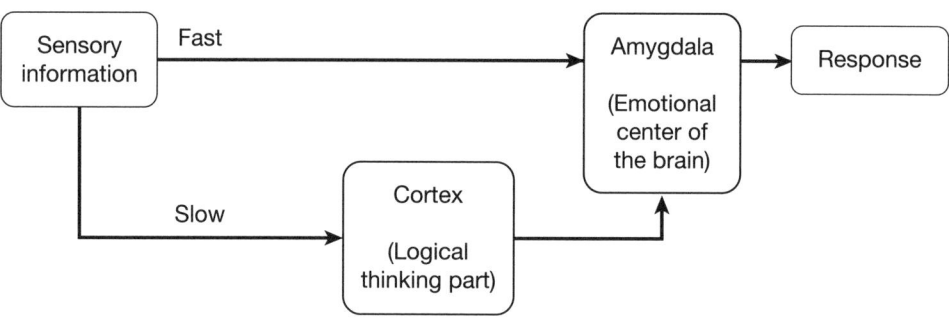

The Amygdala: The Fast Response

The amygdala, part of the limbic system, relates present-moment sensory information to past experience and signals to the rest of the body to react accordingly. It responds very quickly. Among other things, it keeps you safe in dangerous situations.

If the amygdala registers input from the exteroceptive senses that it identifies as similar to as a negative past experience, then it sends signals to release stress hormones for fight, flight, or freeze. For example, when a war veteran hears a loud bang from a car backfiring or a slamming door, they might dive for cover under a table.

Alternatively, when the amygdala receives sensory information that it relates to something pleasant from the past, such as a delivery person arriving with a bouquet of colorful, fragrant flowers, the amygdala sends signals to release hormones that elicit pleasant internal sensations and muscular responses such as a smile.

The Neocortex: The Slower Rational Response

The response from the neocortex comes by a slower information pathway. Information from the sensory nervous system is passed to the cortex via the hippocampus (see the next section). Rather than reacting immediately, as with the amygdala response, the cortex reviews the sensory information with rational thought and problem solving. If the amygdala has responded with fight or flight in the fast response, the cortex will either decide that the amygdala was correct or send information via hormones to the amygdala that the situation is safe and there is no longer a cause for alarm.

For example, if in the past a person has had a difficult or dangerous experience involving an umbrella, upon seeing an umbrella, the amygdala may immediately signal a survival response causing ANS activation (described in Chapter 3). However, once the information reaches the cortex, the person will be able to consider the current situation rationally. When they see that the umbrella is carried by their beloved and trusted brother-in-law who is smiling with open arms to greet them they will realize that this time the umbrella is not a sign of danger.

The Hippocampus: The Link to Clear Thinking

Like the amygdala, the hippocampus is part of the limbic system. It assists in transfer of information between the sensory nervous system and the cortex. When a situation is evaluated as safe, the cortex can then communicate to the amygdala to stop sounding the danger alarm. The hippocampus also adds a time stamp to acknowledge the end of events. When a stressful or dangerous event is over, the hippocampus can halt the warning signal of the amygdala.

However, the amygdala is able continue to function with a high level of released stress hormones, while the hippocampus is not. When the stress or threat level is very high, it is possible for the hippocampus to become suppressed, meaning that it may not be able to communicate information to the cortex. In that case, if a situation is actually safe, per the umbrella example, above, the amygdala might not receive a signal to turn off the danger alarm. Moreover, the hippocampus would not be able to signal that the situation had ended. The result would be that a person would feel as though the threatening event has never ended or is still taking place even when it has long passed. This is a hallmark symptom of PTSD.

The ability to think clearly requires the hippocampus to function properly. Therefore, to be able to think clearly, it is essential to keep stress hormones below the level that would suppress the hippocampus. Likewise, heightened arousal levels that overwhelm the hippocampus and interrupt information flow to the cortex, interfering with clear thinking, are the root cause of a flipped lid.

EXERCISE Identify Your Responses

1. Consider times when you have used the fast and slow responses, as described above.

   a. Consider a time when you experienced the fast (amygdala) and slow (neocortex) responses in a safe situation.

   For example, fast response: I startled in fear when tapped on the shoulder at the dinner party; slow response: I then realized it was a dear friend and that I was safe.

   Fast response: _____

   _____

   _____

   Slow response: _____

   _____

   _____

   b. What sensory information caused the initial stress response?

   Saw: _____

   Heard: _____

   Smelled: _____

   Felt: _____

   Tasted: _____

   c. What were the body sensations of that fast response?

Tight chest	Butterflies in belly	Tense muscles	Faster heartbeat	Fidgety
Stiffness	Numbness	Narrowed eyes	Hot hands	Holding your breath

Breathing fast	Warm feet	Quick movement	Shriek	Sweaty
Any other reactions:				

d. What information helped you to calm down and think clearly?

For example, I looked at the person who had tapped me on the shoulder and saw her smiling face and her arms open wide and recognized her as my best friend.

_____

_____

_____

_____

e. Identify how you felt once you had this information and knew it was safe and you were able to think clearly.

_____

_____

_____

_____

2. Answer questions *a* to *e* below.

a. Identify a time when you felt in danger for an extended period, but in retrospect you were safe.

For example, I suddenly felt my heart beat and breathing quicken and a feeling of panic, when I was sitting at home knitting with the radio on in the background.

_____

_____

_____

_____

b. What caused the initial stress response?

For example, I now realize that there had been mention of a trauma similar to something I have experienced on the news.

_____

_____

_____

_____

c. How intense was that initial stress response?

_____

_____

_____

_____

d. In retrospect, was there any sensory information that could have made its way to your amygdala via the hippocampus if the hippocampus had been online?

_____

_____

_____

_____

e. How able were you to think clearly while you were in the stressful situation?

_____

_____

_____

_____

SELF-HISTORY

Having lived experience of events or circumstances that are similar to a client's can be incredibly beneficial in providing insight that can support compassion and understanding, but the risk of triggering is often high. However, for clear thinking it is essential that the therapist is able to keep their lid on no matter what a client brings to the therapy. When a client is sharing experiences that remind you of your own past, triggering or unmanaged countertransference can make it difficult to think clearly.

For example, if you are a therapist who has experienced violence in childhood, working with a client who is processing violent trauma memories may be a trigger that causes you to remember your own experience as the client describes theirs. If you are unprepared, it could be overwhelming.

Taking a client's history is hopefully something you do regularly to help you have a fuller picture of their life and circumstances as well as to assess what their needs might be, the direction of therapy, what triggers and resources they might have, what you need to look out for, and how might be the best way to support them. Similarly, having a good handle on your own history can help you have a grounded awareness of what might be helpful and what might trigger you. That can support you to feel prepared and aware of the potential for unmanaged countertransference so that you are able to think clearly enough to stay calm and make decisions.

You may have already had personal therapy to process past traumas and difficulties and been through a history-taking process with a therapist. While you may have done a self-history previously with a therapist, new life experiences, as well as the way you feel about old ones, may have since changed. Therefore, regular self-assessment can be useful. This might be whenever you notice a shift, or you may decide to mark in your calendar an annual or biannual check-in.

EXERCISE Your History

1. Complete the table below as though you were taking the history of a client. Note only the titles of incidents rather than expanding into the details of anything, particularly of any traumas.

		Stress?	Stress level 1–10
Current Status and Identity			
Current living situation and relationship status			
Relationship satisfaction			
Any children and ages			
Relationships between the family members			
Physical and mental health of each family member			
Animal companions and their role in your life			
Sex assigned at birth and gender identity			
Ethnicity, heritage, racial identity, and culture			
Nationality and residence status and history			
Education and family history of education			

		Stress?	Stress level 1–10
Class and family history of class			
Sexual identity/ orientation			
Neurodiversity/ neurotypicality			
Language(s)			
Age			
Health			
Your physical and mental health			
Disabilities			
Do you have a diagnosis included in the umbrella term 'neurodiversity'?			
Health history Have you been hospitalized? Had surgery? Major injuries?			

	Stress?	Stress level 1–10
Any serious concerns about mental or physical health		
List the medications you are currently taking, psychotropic and medical; include homeopathic remedies, vitamins, and other supplements.		
What is your drug (legal and illegal) and alcohol history, and your current usage?		
How much caffeine and sugar do you consume?		
If you have or have had bouts of depression or bipolar episodes, are you aware of any patterns? Include planning, attempts, or gestures of suicide.		
Relationships		
List close friends, siblings, family members, and extended family.		
How are these relationships individually?		
On the whole, do you feel adequately supported in your life?		

	Stress?	Stress level 1–10
Are you burdened by responsibilities for family and friends?		
What gives you pleasure with the people in your life?		
What gives you pain?		
Consider the biases and prejudices held by your country/family/culture.		
Work		
Describe your job(s) and your workplace(s).		
Which aspects do you most and least enjoy? What would you change if you could?		
Are there coworkers or responsibilities that give you significant stress?		
If you are in private practice, do you have adequate collegial support? If you work in an agency, do you feel supported there?		

	Stress?	Stress level 1–10
Are you satisfied with your chosen career?		
Do you wish for a different type of work or workplace? What would that be?		
Do you look forward to retirement or not?		
Consider your financial situation. Do you have adequate income, or is this an area of stress for you?		

FAMILY OF ORIGIN

Below is an opportunity to detail your family-of-origin constellation. It involves drawing a chart to see the relationships.

Go back at least two generations if possible, including grandparents (and foster or adopted grandparents where appropriate). Indicate who is alive and who is not. For deceased family members, include how old they were at the time of death and what they died of.

For example, Ursula's chart:

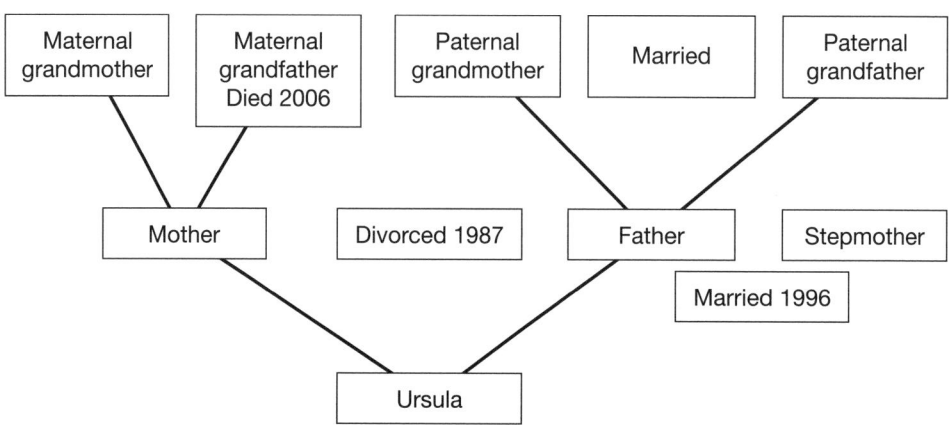

		Stress?	Stress level 1–10
Significant Life Events			
List any life events with significant emotional charge: happy, sad, exciting, frightening, enraging, disgusting.			
List any life-threatening events not covered above (titles and year only).			
List any events of physical or sexual violence not covered above (titles and year only).			

		Stress?	Stress level 1–10
Experiences of oppression/ discrimination/ prejudice.			
Sexual history: Include how you learned about sex, how you managed puberty, first sexual experience, and so on, and your current sexuality.			

		Stress?	Stress level 1–10
Spiritual			
Any spiritual beliefs, whether or not they are part of an organized system.			
Note your relationship with other-than-human-nature.			
Add anything else missed by the previous questions.			

EXERCISE   Identifying Your Potential Sources of Stress

1. While you are noting down your history, notice any stress responses you have to any events. Where you notice that, add a check mark to the "Stress?" column.

2. Then in the next column, rank the stressfulness from 1 (a little stress) to 10 (the most stressed you can imagine).

3. For each of these, consider whether intervention would be useful: for example, whether support from a therapist or other helping professional can offer help, or whether you need to assess how to reduce the likelihood of this decreasing your quality of life. Where you feel that an intervention may be required (this is likely to be the stresses with the highest numerical stress level), list possible actions of support, as in the table below.

Stress (title only)	Action of support
For example, death of grandmother	*Arrange session with therapist; explore options for attending grief support group; not take on any grief-related clients at the moment; discuss in supervision.*

EXERCISE Your Client's History

1. Create the same history table for your clients; you may want to make one for each of your clients, or just for those who are particularly challenging.
2. Use what information you have and do not worry if you do not know the answer for a particular row; you will not be able to fill in all of the rows for all of your clients.
3. It may be possible to fit several or all clients on a single table (with a landscape page or by using Excel or Sheets), or you may want each client to have a separate table.

EXERCISE Identifying Possible Sources of Countertransference

1. Put your own table next to one of the client tables and identify all the rows where you and your client both have similar sources of stress.
2. Identify areas where you both have stress levels of 5 and above, and areas where you both have stress levels of 8 and above. These areas may have a higher risk of out-of-control countertransference.

EXERCISE Strategies for Avoiding Out-of-Control Countertransference

1. Recall the review exercise in Chapter 3 where you listed your most effective calming strategies. Review this and find a calming strategy to use for each of the countertransference risks identified in the previous exercise: one to do before sessions, one during a session, and one to use after a session.

Client: _____

Calming strategy before: _____

_____

Calming strategy during: _____

_____

Calming strategy after: _____

_____

Client: _____

Calming strategy before: _____

_____

Calming strategy during: _____

_____

Calming strategy after: _____

_____

Client: _____

Calming strategy before: _____

_____

Calming strategy during: _____

_____

Calming strategy after: _____

_____

Client: _____

Calming strategy before: _____

_____

Calming strategy during: _____

_____

Calming strategy after: _____

_____

Client: _____

Calming strategy before: _____

_____

Calming strategy during: _____

_____

Calming strategy after: _____

2. Following each session, evaluate the strategies you used. Identify which you will continue to use, which you will adapt or edit, and which you will lay aside. You can make notes on what you discovered here:

_____

_____

_____

EXERCISE   Matching New Clients With Your Current Capacity

Markus took a self-inventory before he took on any new clients. He considered the issues that his current clients were working through and his current competence and capacity for each, as well as how it felt to work with more of that particular issue. The self-inventory highlighted that Markus had a couple of friends who had recently died from terminal illnesses. His grandmother had also been taken ill suddenly, and his family were concerned about her life expectancy. He was currently working with two clients who had recently experienced bereavements, and while he was supporting them well, he felt that he was at the limit of his capacity with regard to working with grief at the moment. He decided that for now he would not take on new clients who wanted to work specifically with grief.

Markus was aware that in the initial consultation sessions, many clients did not yet feel comfortable opening up about the difficulties they were facing. This sometimes meant that he did not know whether the issue he wanted to limit was something that the new client had not yet told him about.

One thing to mitigate this, as well as to reduce overwhelm in clients who conversely wanted to tell everything about their traumas in the consultation, was to ask for titles for life events, stopping clients from recounting details. Markus explained to clients that he was aware that in initial sessions it was difficult to share challenging information, and that it was important to their well-being that they did not tell stories about trauma, especially before they had built a relationship and resources. Markus invited them to say yes or no in response to some general potential life events, along with the year they experienced that, if they wished.

He asked clients, "For example, have you ever experienced the sudden loss of someone close to you? Have you ever witnessed violence?" Markus found that

this method enabled people to be open about their needs and experiences without feeling they had to fully disclose.

Another way he limited the work he took on was to let people know clearly what work he was not offering at the moment in his email responses to people inquiring about therapy and on his website. He stated clearly on his website that he currently had spaces for clients but that he was not currently working with issues directly related to grief.

Of course, things change, and his current clients might unexpectedly experience loss and add to that area of his caseload. In those circumstances Markus spoke with his supervisor to decide whether he had the capacity to offer good therapy with his and his client's well-being in mind, or whether he needed to take steps to refer a client to another practitioner.

These questions can help you decide if you feel stable enough to take clients, based on how their current needs match with your current capacity. It can be important to take into account what issues your current caseload has that you are finding challenging or stressful, to help you know what additional areas you feel most and least able to support people with at the moment.

Of course, some new clients may not feel able to disclose their difficulties at the initial consultation. Additionally, it is potentially retraumatizing for clients to speak at length about a traumatic experience in an initial consultation. Vanessa encourages clients to give only titles of events in these initial consultations so that clients are less likely to get overwhelmed and may feel more able to share their history more easily.

1. Take just the rows from the table you created in the Your History exercise that have the highest stress scores and write them below. Like Markus, you will likely need to revisit this regularly to reassess.

    Areas of high stress for me at the moment are:

    _____

    _____

    _____

    _____

    _____

    _____

    _____

2. Devise some questions to ask potential new clients. These questions should be designed to assess whether new clients could be a source of triggers for you or increase your stress or unmanaged countertransference. That way you can assess whether a client is or is not appropriate.

   For example, "You may wish to answer yes or no to the following questions or let me know that you do not wish to answer that question. You may decide to mention the year(s) when the event happened. Have you ever had a serious trip or fall? Have you ever experienced violence? Have you ever witnessed violence? Has someone close to you died suddenly?"

3. In initial consultations, it is useful to find out what a client wants to gain from therapy and what particular issues are currently difficult for them. While it may be difficult to gain a full understanding of their needs and experiences, it may give an idea of whether the client has areas of focus that would conflict with your current capacity. It is also a great way to start the therapy journey—it can be incredibly difficult to be as useful to someone if you don't have an idea where you are heading.

4. Consider what questions you might ask a client to find out what they want to gain from therapy:

   _____

   _____

   _____

   _____

   _____

DUAL AWARENESS

Clear thinking requires the capacity for a simultaneous awareness of interoceptive and exteroceptive information. Being aware of interoceptors enables you to be aware when you are hungry, need the bathroom, and feel tired. Interoceptive awareness also makes it possible for you to be acutely aware of the subtle signs of ANS activation such as a raise in heartrate or a dry mouth before you flip your lid, so that you can intervene to maintain clear thinking. Exteroceptive awareness enables you to be aware of all sensory information that can alert you to safety and danger in your environment, as well as to be able to distinguish something that might relate to a past trauma or stressful experience from what is happening in the moment.

When the hippocampus, amygdala, and prefrontal cortex are all working optimally, the internal information and external information will line up, enabling good decision-making about a situation. But that is not always easily possible. People with PTSD have a tendency to develop an interoceptive bias, whereby they make decisions about their external reality, including their present safety and danger, based on internal feelings. Therapists who have PTSD or are experiencing vicarious trauma can also experience this.

> *Mehul was eating their lunch in the staff room when suddenly they felt a sense of terror, their stomach and muscles clenched, and they stopped eating mid-bite. Using their exteroceptor of hearing, they noticed that their colleagues were discussing a case of rape, something that Mehul had experienced. Mehul looked around the room and could not see any signs of danger. They noticed their colleagues were now smiling and calmly eating. Mehul could not smell, taste, or feel anything that indicated danger. Mehul realized that their body had responded to what was said, and prepared for danger, as it reminded them of an actual threat from the past. This bodily response had caused Mehul to momentarily believe that they really were in danger. Mehul concluded that while they had felt the body sensations indicative of being in danger, in that moment they were in fact safe.*

While this situation happened when Mehul was in the staff room, it could just as easily have happened during a session when a client described an event that related to Mehul's experience. In this example, Mehul was able to engage their exteroceptive sense of hearing so that they could recognize what had triggered their sense of danger. They were then able to identify that they had heard people talking about danger, rather than actually being in danger in that moment.

Developing the skills of dual awareness, that is, noticing internal sensations and external environment simultaneously, is essential to clear thinking. Practicing this when you feel calm can help you develop this skill so that it is much easier to apply when you are with a client.

The opposite of interoceptive bias can also occur: exteroceptive bias. This involves an acute focus on the external, whereby you lose interoceptive information that alerts you to your own needs. This can be a major risk factor in burnout.

> *Esther was feeling completely exhausted and spoke to her supervisor about how all of a sudden she felt wiped out and was not able to think clearly. Her supervisor asked her how long she had felt exhausted, and when it first started. Esther realized that she wasn't able to identify when the feeling started. Esther described how she was used to noticing the body language and emotional shifts of other people but had difficulty recognizing them in her own body. She had grown up in a household where it had been dangerous not to pay meticulous attention to the changing moods of her mother and to respond quickly to them to keep safe. This awareness meant that she was fantastic at noticing overwhelm in her clients, and was able to help them to regulate their nervous systems before they flipped their lid. However, she realized that the complete focus on the other person was at a cost to her own self-awareness.*
>
> *Esther's supervisor encouraged her to start to explore her own body sensations, taking small steps to identify what increasing tiredness felt like, so that she would be able to respond and take steps to rest before she got to the exhaustion stage.*

When reading the stories of Mehul and Esther, did you identify with one of their situations? If so, then you may have identified whether exteroceptive or interoceptive bias is more likely for you. The first two exercises below begin with exploring and developing awareness in these areas. You might decide to do these no matter your bias, to double check. If you notice a bias, it may be useful to revisit the exercise regularly to increase your awareness.

Some people experience a strong destabilizing response when noticing interoceptive cues. If this applies to you, take it very slowly, exploring how to do this in a way that enables you to keep your lid on, possibly with a therapist. Of course, you also have the option to skip this exercise and not explore your interoceptive cues. Decide what is best for you.

EXERCISE Interoceptive Awareness

1. Similarly to the Check-In exercise in Chapter 3, bring awareness to the different areas of your body, starting with your head and moving your awareness down your body to your feet.
2. Use the diagram below, and suggested vocabulary, to draw or write what you notice in the corresponding place for your body.

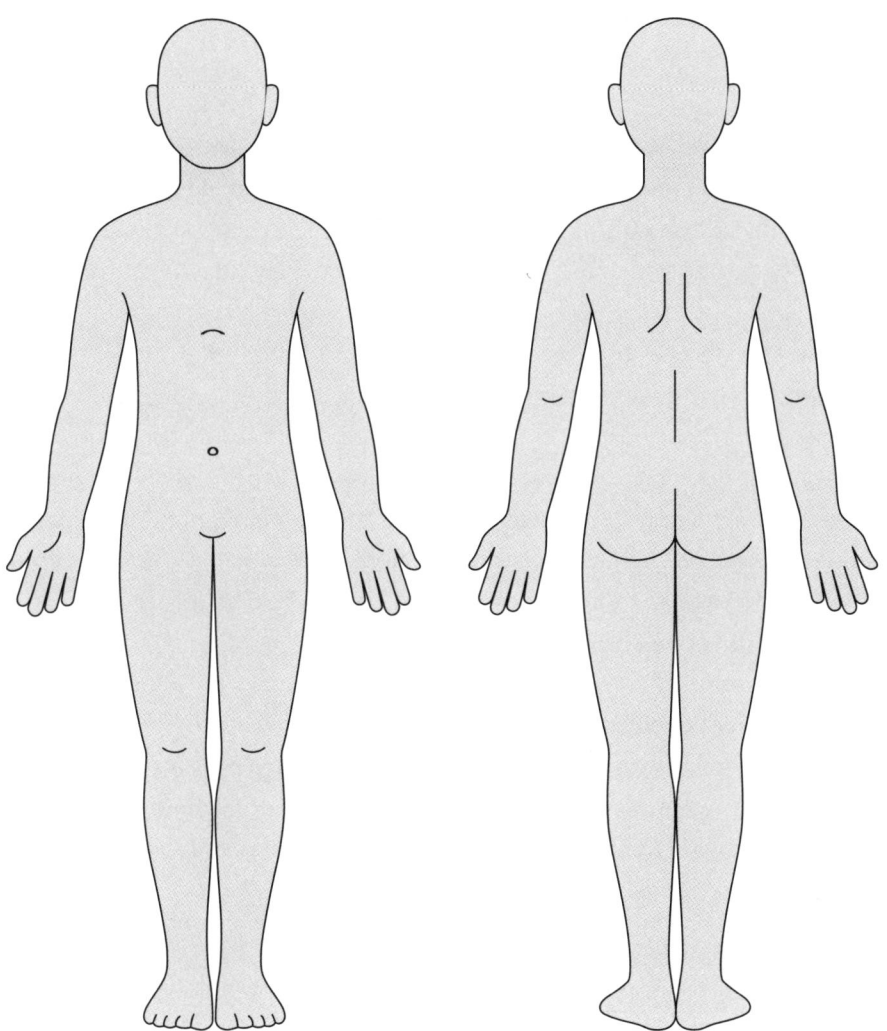

Possible body sensations and feelings; feel free to add more descriptors:

Restless	Tired	Aching	Energized	Numb	Fidgety
Warm	Cold	Hot	Tense	Tight	Fluttering
Soft	Calm	Twitchy	Steady	Frozen	Relaxed
Stiff	Heavy	Light	Dry	Wet	

EXERCISE Exteroceptive Awareness

This exercise is a little like the game *I Spy,* but using all your senses. Play it with a colleague, a friend, or on your own. Once you feel confident, you could share it with a client to help you both have clear thinking during the session. You could set an alarm throughout the day to remind you to take a 30-second break to play this for a minute or so.

1. Choose an exteroceptive sense to focus on and say the first thing you notice: "Right now, I can see/hear/smell taste/feel . . . "
   For example: Right now, I can see red flowers; right now, I can hear someone speaking on the radio; right now, I can feel the roughness of my jumper on my lower arms; right now, I can taste the coffee I drank earlier; right now, I can smell the lavender from the scented candle. Note that "feel" in the exteroceptive context refers to sensations on the skin surface: hot, cold, breeze, and so on.
2. Take turns to notice and say one sense at a time.
3. It can be a bonus to play next to a window or outdoors to get the added benefits of connecting with nature.
4. Doing the exercise with someone else may allow you to notice external information that you had missed. Notice if there is any pattern to what you each notice and miss, in case it would be useful to strengthen your awareness in one or more of your exteroceptive senses.

Practicing Dual Awareness

Dual awareness, awareness of both interoceptor and exteroceptor information, can help you to think clearly so that:

- like Mehul, you are able to differentiate between remembering danger versus actually being in danger in the present;
- like Esther, you are able to maintain awareness of how you are responding to a situation so that you are able to be in control of your well-being.

EXERCISE Dual Awareness

This is similar to the Exteroceptor exercise above, but this time name one exteroceptor and one interoceptor. For example: *Right now, I can hear birds singing and I can feel tension in my forehead; right now, I can see the green leaves of the plant on my desk and I can feel my belly rumbling; right now, I can smell the peppermint tea on the table and I can feel my full bladder.*

1. Name one thing noticed using one interoceptor and exteroceptor.

    Noticed using interoceptor: _____

    Noticed using exteroceptor: _____

2. Either continue noticing one of each for 30 seconds, or play it with a partner, taking turns to name what you notice over an agreed time period.

EXERCISE Practice Dual Awareness at Home

1. Choose an everyday activity for this exercise, such as watching television, reading a book, making and eating food, or walking outdoors.
2. Set an alarm to sound or vibrate every 5 minutes.
3. Each time the alarm sounds, check your interoceptors to identify your internal experience and use your exteroceptors to identify your external environment. It is likely to be easiest to use one interoceptor/exteroceptor set at a time.
4. Continue for the length of the activity, preferably at least 30 minutes.
5. Do this to help you to get used to routinely checking in with yourself and your environment. It may help you to develop this skill so that you can use it when you are working with clients.

EXERCISE Practice Dual Awareness With Others, Part 1

Start with this exercise, then move on to Part 2 when you feel confident.

1. Talk to a friend about something that you both enjoy or a pleasant memory that you both share. Maybe talk about a park that you both really love to visit, or a time you went out for lunch together.

2. Set an alarm to sound every minute.

3. When the alarm sounds, take turns to share an interoceptive sense and an exteroceptive sense, for example, something you feel inside your body and something you notice from the environment.

4. Continue to speak about the pleasant topic, stopping to share dual awareness.

EXERCISE Practice Dual Awareness With Others, Part 2

1. Decide on a mildly stressful event or worry from the last 24 hours to discuss. Ensure that it is mild for both of you. For example, while talking about being served a disappointingly cold coffee might be a mild stress for you, it may be a trigger for your partner, so make sure you agree on it.

2. Agree on an amount of time for the exercise, no more than 3 minutes.

3. Set an alarm to sound every minute.

4. When the alarm sounds, take turns to share an interoceptive sense, such as a body sensation, and exteroceptive sense, something you notice from the environment.

5. Continue to speak about the stressful topic, stopping to share dual awareness, until the final timer sounds, or until you have completed three sets of dual awareness.

6. Consider which calming exercise from Chapter 3 may be useful after talking about the stressful topic.

7. Continue to experiment using a timer until you feel confident in your ability to hold dual awareness without the need for a reminder.

EXERCISE Practice Dual Awareness, Part 3

1. Follow the same steps as the previous exercise, however, this time without a timer to remind you.

2. Choose a different method of practicing dual awareness. Possibly:
   - Continually alternating your awareness between what is said and your interoceptive and exteroceptive awareness.
   - Whenever you hear a common recurring noise, such as bird song, or a car go by, or a door close, check in with dual awareness.
   - Choose a word that is a reminder to check in. Ideally use a relatively common word. For instance, whenever you hear or say "when," you pay attention to dual awareness.

3. If you notice feelings of stress in your body, use your exteroceptors to check whether you are safe or in danger. Take the response seriously: Rather than assuming safety or going through the motions, allow yourself to really check with your exteroceptors that you are safe. If you are not safe, take action to make yourself safe (for example, close the door), or get to safety (for example, flee to a shelter). If you are safe, this practice will help to reassure your system that you are taking the signals seriously and give you an experience of collecting accurate information.

EXERCISE Dual Awareness in Sessions

1. Decide upon a method of dual awareness, possibly from the suggestions in the previous exercise or another that appeals to you. Keep track of its effectiveness.

Method of dual awareness	Effectiveness score (1, worst; 10, best)

2. Monitor your internal feelings during sessions; practice focusing on the client while also remembering to pay attention to what is happening for you internally as well as your external environment.
3. If you start to feel stressed, notice what is going on externally and internally and identify the source of stress. This may be good for a timeout break for both you and your client to check in each with yourself.
4. Keep track of what causes you stress and notice if you are internally or externally biased so that you can practice outside of sessions to balance out the bias.

Common Causes of Stress for Me in Sessions

For example, I feel my stomach tighten and my heart beat faster when my client talks about her controlling mother.

_____

_____

_____

_____

_____

_____

Reducing Identification

When practicing dual awareness, Tani became aware that whenever a client spoke about domestic abuse, her heart rate increased, she felt hot, and she had a feeling of panic. Prior to exploring dual awareness regularly throughout the sessions, she had not linked these feelings of stress with the specific topic. She had simply noticed over time that she was feeling generally tired and stressed.

Tani had grown up in a violent household. She knew what it was like to feel more fear than connection with a family member and had felt that this life experience had enabled her to have deeper understanding for clients who had also experienced this. She felt disheartened that what she had thought was a resource could sometimes also be detrimental to her well-being.

Tani decided that she wanted to know more about it. She started to take more notice of what happened when she began to feel ANS activation in the sessions, using the Check-In exercise from Chapter 3. She noticed that whenever clients were talking about their experiences, she was simultaneously remembering what had similarly happened to her. Unconsciously she had been conjuring images of those scenes of her childhood. In addition, she noticed her self-talk often compared what she heard with her own experiences: "That was just like when my dad . . . "

Tani realized that while her personal understanding of what her client's experience was like and her experience of recovering from PTSD were assets, constantly remembering her traumatic experiences in the sessions was not useful for her or her client.

If, like Tani, you and your client have similar experiences, you may be at increased risk for unhelpful identification with your clients. However, this can still happen when your life experiences are different. Some therapists become at risk when imagining in their mind (visually, auditorily, or feeling in their body) what their clients are telling them. Others notice self-talk like, "That could have happened to me" or "What would that look like if it happened to me?" Identifying with a client's experience in this way is likely to cause ANS activation in a similar way to the response of mirroring discussed in Chapter 2 and can lead to vicarious traumatization.

EXERCISE   Identifying Overidentification

1. Revisit the tables completed in Your History and Your Client's History earlier in this chapter, including all the histories of yourself and your clients.
2. Find the rows where your experiences match.
3. Think of those sessions. What do you say to yourself?
4. During the next session, monitor your self-talk and imagery, consciously taking time to check in with the content of your thoughts as part of your dual awareness. If possible, write these down during the session. If that is difficult to do, note them down immediately afterward.
5. After the session, reflect on your self-talk and imagery—do you overidentify?

Self-talk and imagery noticed	Subject/topic client referring to
For example, imagining rape happening to me	*Client describing sexual assault*
For example, thinking "That reminds me of my attacker"	*Client describing their attacker*

EXERCISE Protector From Self-Identification

If you experience imagining or remembering traumatic or stressful incidents while listening to client traumas, it is likely that you have a good imagination. It can be useful to harness that skill in your favor to support you, rather than in a way that is not helpful.

1. Repeat the word "protector" a few times and notice what immediately comes to mind. It might be a mythical being, a patronus as in the *Harry Potter* books, someone trustworthy from your past, or something connected with nature, such as a mountain range, a river, or the sun.

   Protector: _____

2. Draw, write, or imagine how this protector looks, sounds, smells, feels, moves, speaks as a protector.

   _____

   _____

   _____

   _____

3. Imagine how the protector might respond to protect you from the images of the past or the self-talk that causes you distress. Maybe a river washes the words away, or a dragon sets fire to them, or a giant turns off a TV screen with those images. Write below how you imagine this protective figure responding.

   _____

   _____

   _____

   _____

4. Before using the protector in sessions with clients, practice with a colleague or friend, discussing a very mildly stressful event. If you notice yourself imagining what they are describing or any identifying self-talk arising, imagine the protective figure responding in the way you have described above. It may be useful to reread what you have written above the first few times.

5. Notice if the protector needs to be changed or adapted to feel more powerful or potent, or if you would like to call it something different.

6. Decide how you will remind yourself to use your protector in sessions with clients. For example, you could find an image or an ornament to represent your protector and put it on your desk.

<table>
<tr><td>EXERCISE</td><td>Separation Affirmation</td></tr>
</table>

You could use this alongside or in place of the previous exercise. It is difficult to hold two statements in your mind at the same time. Therefore, repeating a word or phrase that has a positive meaning for you can help to take the place of harmful self-talk. Noticing any positive somatic markers (see Chapter 2) while doing this can strengthen its usefulness. If you use it alongside the previous exercise, you might wish to imagine the protector repeating it along with you.

1. Consider possible affirmations or statements that would be appropriate for you if you notice you are identifying with what a client is saying, something that acknowledges that your experience has similarities but that your client's story is not your story.

2. Write down any possible ideas for this that come to mind:
   For example, "This is similar to my experience, but this is not my story."

   _____

   _____

   _____

   _____

   _____

3. Experiment with saying your affirmations in your mind and perhaps out loud. Put an asterisk next to two that feel most potent and easy to remember.

4. Experiment with using them, noticing which one has the most benefit.

5. Decide how you will remember to use your affirmations. For example, you might write them out on a note and stick them wherever would be easy for you to see when you are in sessions. Or if you are concerned about a client seeing a note, you might prefer to write in code, such as using the first letter of each word. For

example, for "Stop. This is similar to my story but it is not my story," you would write STISTMSBIINMS. While it just looks like a jumble of letters for anyone else, to you who has practiced repeating this affirmation, it will simply be a prompt. Or put the full sentence in a place out of their sight. What other ways might you remember?

REDUCING SELF-CRITICISM

Therapists are not immune to the same types of difficulties that are experienced by their clients and the wider world. Many therapists and helping professionals are wounded healers, with difficulties in their past, including relationships that have involved criticism and critical comparison. While you may have worked through some of these difficulties, when feeling stressed, tired, overwhelmed, or activated, old difficulties can reemerge, including self-criticism.

Self-criticism can be extremely debilitating and can make it very difficult to think clearly. Criticism can become so intense that it can make it very difficult to accept your worth and importance, reducing your ability to prioritize your needs and to set boundaries.

EXERCISE Compassionate Person Interview

The purpose of this exercise is to help you develop a more supportive, compassionate inner voice. It can be useful to do at the start of each week or each day, as well as whenever you notice self-criticism. You can draw, write, imagine, or act out (by sitting in different chairs) the steps of the interview; whatever feels best for you and most appropriate to the setting you are in.

1. Choose a person, or animal companion, from any time in your past, who liked you and was on your side. It might be someone you met fleetingly; it might have been a dog who was constantly by your side throughout your childhood, a best friend, or a partner. It is likely that whoever you choose won't have been perfectly supportive. No one is. Nonetheless, imagine them on their best day, when you felt close and connected with them and they to you. *Caveat:* This should *not* be anyone who has caused you serious harm.

It is most beneficial if this person or companion is someone you have actually known. However, if you can't think of anyone suitable, then you could experiment with using something powerful for you, such as a religious or spiritual figure, or the protector figure from the Protector from Self-Identification exercise in Chapter 4.

2. Imagine that this person is being interviewed. It might be you that is conducting the interview or a third party, such as Oprah Winfrey. You can imagine, draw, write, or speak out loud their responses to the following questions.

3. Consider questions about yourself that would give them an opportunity to speak about you favorably and compassionately. Write the questions in the space for Question below. Caveat: Your person or companion never needs to know about this interview in real life unless you choose to tell them.

   For example, What do you like about [your name]?[Your name] is feeling low levels of self-worth, what do you think about that? Do you have the same or a different opinion? What do you see as [your name]'s qualities?

4. Now imagine how they would answer the question and write or draw or speak aloud their response.

5. If it is difficult to do this, notice if it is possible to remember what they have actually said or done in the past to show that they value you and make a list of those interactions. For example, Jason's uncle, who loved him dearly, but who never said much. Nonetheless, Jason recognized his uncle's love and approval through his hugs, and sometimes just a simple smile or slight nod of his head.

   Question:

   _____

   Answer:

   _____

   _____

   Question:

   _____

   Answer:

   _____

   _____

   Question:

   _____

Answer:

_____

_____

Question:

_____

Answer:

_____

_____

Question:

_____

Answer:

_____

_____

6. Notice your response, maybe using the Check-In exercise from Chapter 3.

7. It may be useful to experiment using different interviewees from your life to assess which has the most positive impact.

EXERCISE Positive Self-Talk Journal

As self-criticism can be engulfing, clear thinking can become so difficult that recalling memories of positive feedback may seem impossible. It might be useful to keep a journal specifically to collect positive feedback you have received recently or in your past so you can remind yourself. Review as a daily or weekly ritual to boost your confidence.

1. Choose a color that represents compassion or positivity for you, and find a notebook or journal in that color. Or open a file in your computer and use that color to write in.

2. Think of positive feedback you have received in the past and write it in the journal. Make sure to include feedback from supportive supervisors, tutors, mentors, therapists, teachers, managers, colleagues, and clients.

3. Continue adding to the journal whenever you get positive feedback from anyone. If clients give you cards or letters with positive words, include those.

4. Keep this journal on your desk or prominent on your computer desktop. Decide whether you will look through it between each client appointment, each lunch break, at the start of each day or week, or simply when you are noticing self-criticism.

5. Notice your response to each piece of feedback, checking for positive body sensations, thoughts, and emotions. If you notice one or more that are particularly potent, you might choose to write it out and display it on your desk or taped to your computer.

EXERCISE Self-Esteem Affirmation

When you notice self-criticism, it can be useful to replace the words with affirmation. In his book *Able and Equal*, Denton Roberts (1987), a transactional analyst, outlines five qualities that he believes contribute to self-esteem and that everyone has the capacity for: to be powerful, capable, valuable, lovable, and equal. With self-criticism it can be difficult to own those qualities in yourself, while as a therapist it is likely that you feel strongly that these are true for the clients that you work with. Roberts's book shares a repeated meditation-style practice to notice your feelings and responses to each of the qualities. The exercise below, uses these qualities as affirmations to repeat when you notice self-criticism.

In between each of the following steps, take a break. Maybe drink some tea or have a walk around, or do them on different days.

1. Reflect on whether you fundamentally believe that everyone has the capacity to be powerful, capable, valuable, lovable, and equal.

_____

_____

_____

2. Repeat the phrase "I am powerful" a few times. Notice how you feel, and write what you notice in your body and what else comes up for you.

_____

_____

_____

3. Repeat the phrase "I am capable" a few times. Notice how you feel, and write what you notice in your body and what else comes up for you.

_____

_____

_____

4. Repeat the phrase "I am valuable" a few times. Notice how you feel, and write what you notice in your body and what else comes up for you.

_____

_____

_____

5. Repeat the phrase "I am lovable" a few times. Notice how you feel, and write what you notice in your body and what else comes up for you.

_____

_____

_____

6. Repeat the phrase "I am equal" a few times. Notice how you feel, and write what you notice in your body and what else comes up for you.

_____

_____

_____

7. Bring it all together. Repeat the phrase "I am powerful, capable, valuable, lovable, and equal" a few times. Notice how you feel, and write what you notice in your body and what else comes up for you.

_____

_____

_____

8. Notice if you'd like to adapt any of the words to best suit your values. For example, "lovable" may become "likable" or "I am" might become "I and all others are ..."

   You may decide to completely change them to something that suits you better that you have heard from a loved one or seen in a movie or book. For example, in the movie *Cool Runnings*, Junior looks in a mirror and repeats the words, "I see pride! I see power! I see a bad-ass mother who don't take no crap off of nobody!"

   _____

   _____

   _____

9. Repeat the words in your mind, or aloud, or write it down a few times.
   Affirmation:

   _____

   _____

   _____

10. Notice any response: body sensations, thoughts, emotions, and whether you need to adapt the phrase in any way.

    _____

    _____

    _____

11. Decide whether this is useful or not for you and, if it is, when you will use it. Maybe writing it on the top of your notebook or on a sticky note on your mirror.

CONTAINER FOR CLEAR THINKING

Sometimes a client that a therapist is working with continues to be on their mind after the session, creating a difficulty in being able to rest, enjoy social activities, or be present with other clients. In that case, a common intervention, often used to help clients, can be helpful for the therapist. Have you helped a client manage stressful or traumatic memories and feelings by imagining putting them into a container for a period of time or between sessions? This exercise utilizes that idea, but for therapists to put concerns about their client work in a secure container.

While the exercises below offer a suggestion, you might already have a preferred method that you use with clients that you might experiment with using yourself.

EXERCISE Container Imagery

In this exercise you can utilize your imagination and creativity to create a container that can hold client work between sessions.

1. Imagine a container that could hold all the feelings, emotions, body sensations, words, and stories that might be shared by your client.
2. Imagine, and then write or draw below:

   What it looks like

   _____

   _____

   What it is made from

   _____

   _____

   How it is held together

   _____

   _____

   How it locks and unlocks

   _____

   _____

   How it is soundproofed

   _____

   _____

   How it is protected: maybe by a force field or by creatures, animals, or beings who can stop things from escaping

   _____

   _____

The environment it is in; for example, in space, at the bottom of the ocean, in a forest

_____

_____

```
┌─────────────────────────────────────────────────┐
│                Draw your container:               │
│                                                   │
│                                                   │
│                                                   │
│                                                   │
│                                                   │
│                                                   │
│                                                   │
│                                                   │
│                                                   │
│                                                   │
│                                                   │
│                                                   │
│                                                   │
│                                                   │
└─────────────────────────────────────────────────┘
```

3. Imagine bundling up the case information about each client and putting it into the container. It might be useful to imagine a way that you can put things into the container without other things escaping.

4. Consider whether you would like to say a phrase as you close and lock the container or give instructions to the protectors of the container. For example, "I am putting this in the container until I decide to open it again," or "Make sure that nothing is removed or escapes from the container until I say so."

5. Imagine saying goodbye to the protectors and imagine where you will leave the key.

6. To reinforce this, it may be important to imagine taking the client information from the container before each session, and then putting it back afterward.

7. If client material comes to mind, imagine putting it back in the container.

EXERCISE Physical Container

In addition to, or in place of, imagining a container, you can develop conscious mindful awareness of locking or shutting down a physical container where your client information and notes are kept, such as a filing cabinet or lockable box, or by closing down the computer file.

1. Consider how you currently store your client notes, any creative work, and other information. If you do not already keep it in a lockable container, consider getting one. If you use computer storage, you may wish to either do this exercise as you close down the program, or you might prefer to find an ornament or pebble to represent each client and use a jewelry box or other container to put them in.

2. At the beginning of each client or supervision session, mindfully say to yourself that you are taking out the client files and notes.

3. After the session, when you have completed any notes and any future session planning for the client, mindfully put all the notes into the container, stating this client information will be locked in here until the next session, or your next supervision.

YOUR WORKSPACE

Jasper worked in a busy counseling service where therapists worked in different sites on different days. Though he was always in the same room on the same day, other therapists used the room at other times. When he worked in one particular room, he noticed that he found it difficult to focus and think clearly. He found his eyes drawn to the piled-up boxes on shelves and felt irritated and agitated by the clutter in the room. When he shared this with his supervisor, they asked him to describe the room and how it differed from the others.

Jasper groaned in response and said that it was a much smaller room than the others, with a view that looked out onto another building. He had to have the blinds drawn and the harsh overhead fluorescent lights on. He described how the room didn't have adequate storage, and so the bookshelves were crammed with different-sized boxes full of art materials and different resources. The chairs were too soft and gave the feeling that he was sinking into them, and the table had different ornaments, potpourri, and plastic flowers that irritated him. Most irritating was that there was no place to put his own files.

His supervisor asked him to describe what kind of workspace would best support his clear thinking. Jasper said that in another room he used the space was quite minimal, with a large window that looked over a field and woods, and provided lots of natural light. Jasper described how looking out of the window at the natural scene helped him to feel calm during and between sessions. He described how the cupboards in that room were fitted with doors so whatever was in the cupboards didn't bother him because he couldn't see it.

At the counseling service Jasper did not have the freedom of being able to change aspects of the room according to his individual tastes and would be unlikely to get any budget to make changes. His supervisor helped him to assess what was within his control to change and whether there were any alternatives to what he would prefer the room to look like. He decided to talk to his manager about adding inexpensive thrift store lamps and changing the seating in the room. He also asked if he could hang a picture featuring a natural scene on the bare walls of the room; not quite the lovely view from the other room, but a good-enough alternative. He also rearranged the table and new chairs so that they did not look toward the unsightly shelving.

Jasper decided to purchase a collapsible box that he could use to store all the unsightly items on the table whenever he used the room, putting it all back at the end of the day. After the first session with these changes, Jasper noticed he was much more able to think clearly in the room. While there were still some things that he would not choose, it was good enough.

The wrong workspace can make it hard to think clearly. What is optimal is very individual. Some people, like Jasper, find a clear, simple space the easiest to think clearly in; others find this empty and like to surround themselves with attractive objects and decorations. The exercises below aim to help you assess whether your workspace affects your capacity for clear thinking, and to consider ways to improve it.

EXERCISE What Workspace Works Best for You?

As you read about Jasper's experience, did you notice whether his workspace would affect you similarly or differently? Consider and answer the following questions to explore what kinds of workspaces support your clear thinking.

1. Picture working in each of the environments described in the tables below. It may help to do a web search to find images of such workspaces.
2. Notice how you would feel working there, circle any of the words below that would apply, and add any more that you notice.
3. Think of other styles of room and see how you would feel in them. Try to identify what you like and do not like and then, through trial and error, try to think of your perfect room. Consider:
   a. Size
   b. Color
   c. Decoration and ornaments
   d. Light
   e. Furniture style
   f. Furniture arrangement
   g. Windows and view
   h. Storage

A room that is very minimalist, neutral colors, with no ornaments and very little decoration						
Calm	Organized	Clinical	Agitated	On edge	Distracted	Cozy
Reassured	Clear-headed	Inspired	Creative	Comfortable	Focused	At ease
Positive features						
Negative features						

A room that has brightly colored walls, pictures, and different ornaments and decoration on the shelves						
Calm	Organized	Clinical	Agitated	On edge	Distracted	Cozy
Reassured	Clear-headed	Inspired	Creative	Comfortable	Focused	At ease
Positive features						
Negative features						

A room with an antique wooden desk and bookshelves, neutral-colored walls, and classic-style lamps						
Calm	Organized	Clinical	Agitated	On edge	Distracted	Cozy
Reassured	Clear-headed	Inspired	Creative	Comfortable	Focused	At ease
Positive features						
Negative features						

A room with a large window overlooking a natural scene, with lots of plants, pictures of nature, and simple wood furniture						
Calm	Organized	Clinical	Agitated	On edge	Distracted	Cozy
Reassured	Clear-headed	Inspired	Creative	Comfortable	Focused	At ease
Positive features						
Negative features						

Other option:						
Calm	Organized	Clinical	Agitated	On edge	Distracted	Cozy
Reassured	Clear-headed	Inspired	Creative	Comfortable	Focused	At ease
Positive features						
Negative features						

EXERCISE   Assess Your Current Workspace

1. Sit in your current workspace. How is it similar and how is it different from the style of workspace you have identified as most positive for you?

   Similar: _____

   _____

   _____

Different: _____

_____

_____

2. As you sit in your room, notice what feels good and what doesn't feel good. Consider:

   • Does it feel too full or too empty?
   • Does it feel too cluttered or too sterile?
   • Is the chair comfortable?
   • Does the chair support you to work or to fall asleep?
   • Does it feel too bright or too dark?
   • Do you prefer separate areas to work at the computer and sit with clients, or to use a desk for both, or neither?
   • Is the storage appropriate?
   • Does it feel personal enough to feel relaxing or cozy, or too personal?

Likes	Dislikes

3. Consider what you have written in the Dislikes section.

    a. What would you change? _____

4. If, as for Jasper, it is difficult to make changes to the room, what compromise or interim changes could you make? For example, Jasper brought a box to put the clutter into while he worked there. Other suggestions include:
   - Bring a picture to put on the desk.
   - Set up an aromatherapy diffuser.
   - Bring a small plant with you.
   - Move some of the clutter and furniture into another section of the room. Bring a side lamp with you with a brighter or dimmer bulb and use that instead of the main light.

Dislikes	Ideal change	Compromise or interim change

| EXERCISE | Office Layout |

> *Whenever Seren went with her friend to her local coffee shop, she hoped that the table by the window at the back would be available. She noticed that when she sat with her back to the door, she felt very distracted and kept wanting to turn around and to see who had entered. It was a stronger feeling for her than simple curiosity; it affected her sense of calm and safety and she lost focus of what she and her friend were talking about. From her preferred table, she could see with her peripheral vision who came in and out without it taking too much of her attention.*
>
> *Similarly, when she had first started working in her new office, it was set up so that the door was to the left and a little behind her desk. Though she posted a Do Not Disturb sign during sessions, whenever she heard someone walk by she felt distracted and automatically turned to look at the door. Talking to a colleague about this, they agreed to help her to move the furniture around so that she could look toward the door. That new arrangement helped her to feel calmer and she was no longer distracted by people walking by.*

This exercise is the next step after the Identify Your Chair and Give Yourself Space exercises in Chapter 3. In those exercises you assessed the best place to put your chair. Here is an opportunity to explore your whole office layout.

Many people have a preferred place to sit in a room. Some like to be beside a window or door; others like to be facing a window, so that they can look outside from time to time. Office layout might make a big difference to your ability to think clearly.

1. Consider the following statements and check any that feel true for you. Consider where you tend to prefer to sit in your living room at home, where you prefer to sit in a restaurant or café, and where in a meeting room you would rather be positioned. It might be useful to check these out through your week.

   I am most able to be focused and think clearly when I sit (check all that apply):
   - ☐ Near a door
   - ☐ Facing a door
   - ☐ With my back to a door
   - ☐ Near a window
   - ☐ Facing a window
   - ☐ Facing away from a window

☐ Directly opposite someone

☐ At a 45-degree angle to someone

☐ Behind a desk

☐ With a small table between me and someone else

☐ With no furniture at all between me and the other person

☐ Other:_____

☐ Other:_____

☐ Other:_____

☐ Other:_____

☐ Other:_____

☐ Other:_____

2. Draw the outline of your office or therapy room below. Mark where the windows and doors are located. *For example:*

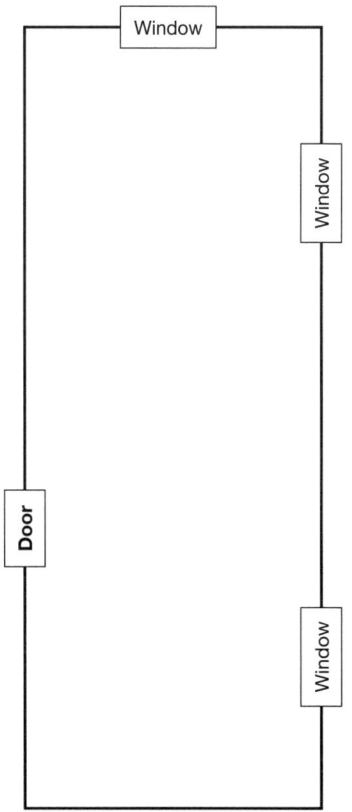

Draw your outline here:

3. Cut out paper to represent chairs, desks, and other furniture you have or would like to add (where possible). As far as possible, do this to scale. Move the paper furniture around the template and in each position imagine being in the room with the layout that way. Notice whether you would feel more or less calm and able to focus.

4. When you find the layout that has the biggest calming response, rearrange your actual room to match as close as possible.

5. Check whether being physically in your room has the same effect as when you imagined being there. Do you need to make any changes?

EXERCISE   The Right Style of Chair for You

In addition to the design and appearance having an effect on clear thinking, the furniture itself can have an impact. Jasper mentioned that the chairs in his room were too soft and that he felt as though he sank into them.

This is a common feeling. It tends to be much easier to be present and calm in seats that offer firm support that enables you to sit upright, with feet flat on the floor. Though of course you want to aim for comfort as well as support, sometimes a slight amount of discomfort, such as a slightly too hard chair, can be useful for staying present and may help keep you from dissociating. Actually, the same can also be a good idea for clients: Have them sit upright in chairs that are slightly too hard as it may also help them to stay more present.

1. Sit in your usual office chair.

    Consider the following:

    a. Does the chair support you to easily sit upright with a straight back? Or does it cause you to slump?

    b. Are your feet able to be flat on the ground?

    c. Is the chair so uncomfortable that it is too distracting? Are you constantly shifting position to find comfort?

    d. Is the chair so comfortable that it is too relaxing? Do you feel sleepy or dissociated?

    e. What else do you notice about the chair?

2. If you find that your chair is impacting your ability to think clearly, it might be useful to take the list of considerations above, and any others you can think of, and visit a furniture store. Try out many different chairs, noticing which would offer the most support for clear thinking.

EXERCISE Separating Work and Home When Working From Home

Sam left his salaried job to work in private practice. After looking at a variety of expensive offices that did not meet his needs, he decided that working online from home was going to be the optimal solution for him.

Sam lived with his partner, Alice, in a one-bedroom apartment that had a separate living room and kitchen. He decided to use a desk that was in a corner of the living room. To ensure confidentiality, Sam decided to only have office hours when Alice was at work. He also moved personal photographs and other personal items that could be seen when videoconferencing.

After working online for a week, Sam found that he was often thinking about his clients when relaxing in the evenings. Speaking to his supervisor, he realized that since he started working at home, he found it more difficult to separate work life from home life. Sam and his supervisor discussed ways that Sam could make a more clear separation. He decided to have a daily ritual to "arrive" at work by first going outside for a short walk and coming in the door saying, "Now I'm at work." He would then turn on the computer to start work. He had a similar ritual at the end of the day, closing the computer down while saying aloud, "That's the end of my work today." He would then go outside for another short walk, and then let himself back in the door announcing "I'm home."

Sam also decided to designate a particular mug for his tea while at work. He also used a different lighting arrangement: a big lamp on the desk while working, that he switched off at the end of his work day. During non-working hours, he would use other mugs and lamps. Sam also decided on different clothing when at home and when at work.

With these rituals, Sam found that separating home from work was possible and noticed a huge reduction in thinking about clients outside of working hours.

1. If you work from home, consider the changes you might make that may help you to separate work time from home time. Like Sam, you might use separate lights, mugs, and clothes for when you're working and when you're not.

Area of home	When working	When not working
For example, lighting	*Use desk lamp*	*Switch off desk lamp and use other lamps*
For example, scent	*Use lavender scent in aromatherapy diffuser*	*Use any scent other than lavender in aromatherapy diffuser*

2. Consider whether a ritual, like Sam's mantra at the start and end of work or when he is leaving and reentering his house, would be useful for you. If so, what would your ritual be?

   Rituals to start the working day:

   For example, leave and reenter the house with mantra, "I am starting work."
   For example, change the lighting and the scent.

   _____

   _____

   _____

   _____

   _____

   _____

Rituals to end the working day:

For example, leave and reenter the house with mantra, "I am going home."

For example, turn off the computer, saying, "That's the end of my

working day."

_____

_____

_____

_____

_____

_____

3. Continue to monitor and tweak the adjustments you have already decided on that help you to maintain clear thinking moment to moment and day to day. Be alert for additional strategies you can utilize from books and colleagues, and develop from your own creativity.

Self-Care During Shared Community/World Crises

Previous chapters have added to your self-care toolbox for working with clients who have faced or are facing difficulties both similar and different from your own. This chapter focuses on self-care when you and your client are simultaneously experiencing the same trauma or crisis. That might include, for example, coping with a pandemic, living in a country or community at war or under some type of oppression, surviving a natural disaster such as a wildfire or an earthquake, and so on. Also, in this chapter time and case management will be considered, which are important at all times but can become even more important during times of crisis.

COMMUNITY AND WORLD CRISES

These larger crises include wars, pandemics, community traumas such as mass murders, experiencing racism, and being part of an oppressed population.

While both authors have experienced types of discrimination, community upheaval, and a pandemic, and are living in current ecological and political crises, we lack personal experience in some areas of shared crisis, such as war. Though we hope that this chapter, as well as this book, gives you a wealth of support, we nevertheless encourage you to seek out additional expertise from those most familiar with the particular crises you are currently facing.

It is particularly challenging when both client and therapist are simultaneously experiencing the same crisis. There can be difficult decisions such as determining boundaries of self-disclosure, how to assess one's fitness to practice, and what the content of sessions should be. Additionally, it may be that while your experiences are similar in some ways, in others they are not.

> *Renée's country had unexpectedly and suddenly come under attack. While Renée lived and worked hundreds of miles away from the bombings, which were currently on the other side of the country, she was feeling extremely fearful. Unsure whether to cancel clients or to go to work, she decided to go. She felt overwhelmed sitting at home and felt a need to be helpful.*
>
> *Her first client of the day came into the room in tears. Renée assumed it was about the attacks, yet when the client sat down, they told her about how they had just split up with their partner. Renée found it incredibly difficult to stay focused on the client's immediate needs, distracted by her own fears of the bombings becoming more widespread. Renée was hot and fidgety and had difficulty feeling compassionate toward her client.*
>
> *Realizing that while other clients might have a need to talk about the attacks, as well as their other difficulties, Renée assessed that she would not be able to be a present and grounded therapist that day. After the first session, she called her other clients to let them know she was taking the day off, and recommended they each connect with loved ones. She then went home to make contact and be with her own supportive network of family and friends.*

The sense of urgency that comes with a crisis can make it difficult to slow down, and create a desire to try to fix everything as quickly as possible. Many become almost desperate to be helpful. All too often, that leads to forgetting one's own needs. A good reminder comes from first aid trainings. The first instruction upon noticing an injured or incapacitated person is "Stop! And assess for danger." First aid students are drilled in checking the environment to ensure their own safety before even approaching an injured person. Another reminder, as written in the first chapter: If an airplane loses pressure, make sure to put on your own oxygen mask first.

While your work is valuable, checking for your own safety and needs first is imperative to be able to be of any help. While Renée truly wanted to support her clients, she quickly realized that what she needed first was to help herself.

| EXERCISE | Stop and Assess Capacity |

Really anytime, but particularly in situations of crisis, it is important to take time before seeing clients to check in with yourself to assess whether you are fit to work that day.

1. Use the Self Check-In exercise from Chapter 3. Ask yourself the questions below: While imagining sitting with the clients scheduled for today:
   - Will I be able to feel present and grounded and focus on their needs today?
   - Am I feeling healthy enough in my body?
   - If I am feeling unwell (and seeing clients in person), am I potentially going to make my clients ill?
   - Am I a good enough mirror today? If my client mirrors me today, will they feel more calm or more dysregulated?
   - Am I feeling energetic enough?
   - Do I have the capacity to employ different strategies to stay calm and appropriately boundaried?
   - Am I likely to end the day feeling burnout or suffering from compassion fatigue?
   - Are there some clients whom I have capacity for today and some clients that I do not?
2. Are there any other questions you would like to use to assess for danger? These could relate to your current situation or past experiences.

_____

_____

_____

_____

_____

YOUR EXPERIENCE

If much of your work is focused on your client's experience of traumatic events, it can be easy to lose connection to your own experience and feelings. Insofar as it affects your day-to-day quality of life, it is useful to reflect on your own experience of world crises.

EXERCISE Your Past Experience

1. If you have ever experienced a world or community crisis:
   a. Did you notice any signs that you were struggling?
      For example, my usual calming strategies were not as potent; I got ill much more often than usual.

   _____

   _____

   _____

   b. What would you have done differently regarding your well-being?
      For example, I wish I had taken more time off; I wish I had prioritized my own needs more.

   _____

   _____

   _____

   c. Reflecting on that time, what helped you cope?
      For example, having an emergency plan and bag packed so that I knew exactly what to do and where to go; support from other members of my community; accessing practical support as well as emotional.

   _____

   _____

   _____

EXERCISE Naming Your Current Experience

In their book *The Whole-Brain Child*, Dan Siegel and Tina Payne Bryson (2012) describe the importance of "Name it to tame it." They describe how, by naming what you are experiencing, you are bringing online your prefrontal cortex, getting your lid back on and helping you to feel less overwhelmed. Having an awareness of your current circumstances can also help you to evaluate the challenges you face, taking them seriously and increasing self-compassion.

1. What world crises are currently affecting you?

_____

_____

_____

2. What community crises are currently affecting you?

_____

_____

_____

3. How do these affect you at the moment? Including whether directly, indirectly, emotionally, psychologically, physically, or socially.
   For example, I feel scared to walk around my neighborhood; I feel overwhelmed whenever I watch the news.

_____

_____

_____

HELPLESSNESS

It's not possible to constantly hone in on the crisis. You have to have the love, and you have to have the magic, that's also life. —Toni Morrison (1977)

Feeling Helpless and Out of Control

Trauma happens when we are not in control. When working with children who have experienced trauma, Vanessa recommends that parents offer their children choices as often as possible so that they are able to get a sense of being in control. For example, "Shall we tidy the toys away while dancing to music, or shall we do it as if we are puppies?"; or "Do you want to eat your peas with a fork or with a spoon?" Similarly, notice when there are options can also help adults feel more in control.

When Renée spoke with her therapist, she described how scared she felt about the attacks and that she felt like there was nothing she could do. She felt

trapped, like a sitting duck. The fear of the attack itself was incredibly wor-
rying, but the feeling of helplessness felt even more painful. She said that she
had noticed her whole body feeling tense and she felt drawn to watching the
news constantly, as if knowing every detail of what was going on could help
her feel more in control.

EXERCISE Assess Your Relationship With
Being Out of Control

Everyone finds the experience of being out of control different. It can be useful to
reflect on your own experience of a lack of control.

1. What is your relationship with helplessness and feeling out of control?

_____

_____

_____

2. What is your usual response to that feeling?
   Body

_____

   Thoughts

_____

   Actions

_____

Taking Control, and Realizing What You Cannot Control

Renée's therapist validated her feelings, saying that no wonder it felt scary to feel
so helpless. Her therapist shared that she had also felt afraid about the attacks.
Speaking about it with her therapist and getting a validating and compassionate
response helped to soothe her. They explored some techniques that Renée could use
to help her to find calm. She noticed that using her exteroceptors to simply look
around the room, listen, be present with the current external reality of the current
moment was the most powerful way to recognize when she was actually safe (even

if temporarily) and distinguish those moments from the moments when she actually was in danger.

Renée's therapist wondered whether there were any ways that Renée could increase her sense of control in her life. They made a list of the things that were in her control when it came to her own and her community's well-being. These included having a bag packed ready in case she needed to leave her home, and creating a phone message group where people could share any alerts, and a separate one where they shared resources and support. For example, Renée's neighbor sent a message inviting everyone to come pick and eat apples from the tree in her garden.

Additionally, Renée realized that though she could not control the news, she could, indeed, be in control of how and how much she was inundated by it. Instead of watching it constantly, she decided she would only read or listen to the news, limiting her exposure to twice per day. When she felt the urge to watch, she would recognize this as a sign that she needed soothing and instead would call a friend or do other calming activities.

She also confirmed other areas of control of her life: That she would keep contact with her therapist and her family and friends, continue to eat healthily, take a little time off work, and that she could participate in the community gardens, where she felt a sense of community, wonder, beauty, and hope.

EXERCISE   Control What Can Be Controlled

1. Consider the resources you already have. What do you already do that helps you feel more in control?

   For example, doing strength exercises, eating healthily, keeping the house tidy, helping others.

   _____

   _____

   _____

   _____

   _____

Of course, no matter how much you may enjoy being part of an empowered community and working toward a healthier and happier world, no one can fix all of the world's problems. This can be disheartening at times, particularly in times of crisis. There may be quotes or poems or strategies that you already use to help keep you feeling calm and motivated when considering this dilemma. For example, Vanessa likes to read poems by Mary Oliver, as well as other, mostly well-known quotes from personal growth and spiritual sources.

2. Which authors and quotes do you find particularly supportive or heartening in difficult times?

_____

_____

_____

_____

_____

EXERCISE Identify and Manage What Cannot Be Controlled

---

1. Consider the resources you already have. What helps when you are not able to change things at all or as quickly or as expansively as you would wish?
   For example, reminding myself that time passes and things change; grounding exercises; connecting with loved ones.

_____

_____

_____

_____

_____

2. Choose a specific situation and consider what parts of that situation could be within your control, and which parts are not. Would it be helpful to find acceptance, or self-forgiveness, that you cannot change things as quickly as you wish? Are there parts of the situation that cannot be changed now, but might be possible in the future? What is not currently in my control to change right now?

_____

_____

_____

3. What could possibly be in my control in the future?

_____

_____

_____

EXERCISE Somatic Expression of Strength and Acceptance

This exercise is designed to help you to feel both strength and relaxation in your hands, but you are welcome to choose another part of your body if that feels better for you. Make sure to read through the exercise before you do it. It might or might not be right for you at this point in time.

1. Stand, sit, or lie down.
2. Make a fist with each hand, noticing the activation of your muscles.
3. You may wish to say an affirmation like, "I am strong and can change some things."
4. Allow your hands to open and your arms and hand muscles to relax.
5. See if it feels right to repeat an affirmation like, "I am learning to let go and to accept that I cannot change everything." Or create your own affirmation.
6. If it feels okay, move between these two opposing states, noticing how it feels.

EXERCISE You Too Are Human

A common judgment among helping professionals is that they shouldn't be vulnerable or feel what their clients feel. There is an erroneous belief that they should somehow be immune to panic and overwhelm or at least be able to immediately become calm and solve their problems. However, just as professional sports coaches can break a bone and need time to heal their bodies and doctors can become ill, so too do mental health professionals experience mental health issues that take time, and sometimes their own therapy, to recover from. All helping professionals, also you, are human too.

1. In the space below, write any words or self-talk that come to mind that echo this belief that therapists (or you) should be immune to mental health problems.

2. In the space below each of those statements, write a response from a compassionate perspective. Consider what you might say or write to a dear friend who worried that they, as a helping professional, shouldn't be affected in the way that they are.

Words or self-talk

_____

_____

Response from compassionate friend

_____

_____

Words or self-talk

_____

_____

Response from compassionate friend

_____

_____

Words or self-talk

_____

_____

Response from compassionate friend

_____

_____

3. Make a plan for how you will compassionately counter these and other self-critical thoughts when they arise.

Control Your Intake of Disturbing Information

The risks you face working with clients such as mirroring, facial feedback, having mental images of what you are hearing, and self-talk such as "That could have been me" or "What if it were me?" are similar with disturbing news exposure whether seen, heard, or read.

Like Renée, you may notice that the constant news cycle during a world or community crisis can be overwhelming. Often, people feel pulled to consume as much news as possible, as though not doing so means they do not care or that they might miss a key piece of information. However, as discussed in previous chapters, when overwhelmed you are less likely to be able to process information or be able to act or think in a way that is useful and rational. Limiting your exposure to news may be important in helping you to keep your lid on.

All exposure to distressing news will put you at risk. However, watching distressing news, as opposed to reading or listening to it, can put you at greater risk through mirror neurons and facial feedback, as described in Chapter 2. That can make you more vulnerable to feeling similar emotions and having parallel body responses as the people you are watching on the news. It can affect you as though you are personally experiencing what they are. As explored regarding clients, this is unlikely to be useful to you. Monitoring your facial expression and body posture and purposely changing both may reduce the effect. Another option is to explore if listening or reading the news is less activating for you than seeing it.

EXERCISE	Set Boundaries for Information Intake During a Crisis

1. Make a list of the pros and cons of taking in information about a crisis currently happening in the world or in your community.

Pros	Cons

2. Reflect on how the ways in which you access the news cycle affect you. In the table below, write any observations, such as whether you notice yourself imagining what you see happening to you, or any unhelpful self-talk such as "That could be me."

	Television	Radio	Social media	Written/ newspaper article
Emotion/body sensations				
Self-talk				
ANS state, e.g., fight, flight, freeze, or calm response				

3. Based on your findings in the table above, which is the method of news intake that is least distressing to you?

_____

4. Consider whether the time of day when you access the news affects how you respond to it. For example, if your wake-up alarm is set to a news radio channel, how does that affect your day compared to if you read the news at a set time each day when you have time to digest what you have read?

When would be the ideal time to access news to reduce negative impact?

_____

5. Consider what your purpose is for reading the news.

What will you do with the information?

_____

_____

If you identify a particular purpose or intention, is it possible to limit your intake to meet this intention? For example, to just watch or read the news summary.

_____

6. After reflecting on how your consumption of information and news affects you, consider what boundaries you might want to put in place for yourself. Check and comment next to the suggestions we have made here and add any others in the spaces.

☐ In times of crisis, I will delete social media apps from my phone to prevent absent-mindedly scrolling through disturbing images.

☐ Set social media favorites so that I can only scroll through certain accounts that I know are unlikely to feature disturbing images.

☐ Change my wake-up alarm to music rather than news.

☐ Limit my news intake to _____ minutes, _____ times per day / week at _____a.m./p.m. on _____(day, if weekly).

☐ Limit my news intake to radio / television / social media / written articles.

☐ Limit news intake to just the summary.

☐ Get the news summary from a friend or partner who gets much less affected by it than I do.

☐ Arrange a calming activity for after I have accessed the news, such as:

_____

☐ Ensure that I am feeling "adult" before I access the news cycle.

_____

_____

_____

TIME MANAGEMENT

Time Off

During the COVID-19 pandemic, Toby's country enforced a lockdown that only allowed people to leave their home for a set amount of time each day and limited their contact with others. Toby had to move client sessions online or on the phone and use his home office to conduct sessions.

Usually, Toby took at least a week of vacation every 6–8 weeks and found that this schedule enabled him to feel rested enough to avoid compassion fatigue and burnout. Each year he additionally took a four-week break in August, a time when many clients were also away on vacation, to fully recharge.

Because of the COVID restrictions, Toby was frustrated that he would not be able to take his usual long break in the sunny seaside spot that he usually enjoyed. He felt disappointed and continued to work through the weeks that he would usually have been off work. He could see no option but to keep working. Initially, he did not take the usual month off because he thought that the pandemic would likely be over after a few weeks, and he thought he would be able to rebook his favorite resort. He was also mindful that his clients would have greater need for ongoing sessions during this difficult quarantine time. However, a few weeks of lockdown turned into a few months, and then a year, and he still had not taken any time off.

During an online peer supervision group, a colleague, Tania, announced that she couldn't make the next session because she would be on vacation. Toby was shocked and a little envious. He asked Tania how she had managed to plan a vacation. Tania shared that she was not going to travel. Instead, she had decided to create a yoga retreat vacation at home. She would camp in her garden, follow online yoga classes, eat her favorite delivered meals, and have online gatherings with her dearest friends.

Toby was inspired—he had not even considered anything like that as an option. Though it would be very different from his beach vacation, he started to imagine what he could do instead. However, he continued to feel guilty about taking vacation time when many of his clients were having such difficulties, and also worried about how they might judge him.

Toby spoke with Tanya about his concerns, asking for advice about how she told her clients about the vacation time. Tania admitted that she too had initially worried, but that she also felt she had an opportunity to model self-care and self-respect to her clients by taking time off. Tania said that she noticed early signs of compassion fatigue and burnout in the early weeks of the pandemic that were stronger than she had ever experienced in the past. She realized that if she was going to have capacity to work well and maintain professional integrity, she would need to take more, not less, vacation during this time.

A common occurrence in crises is that therapists can find it difficult to take time off. As for Toby, it may seem impossible at first, but there will likely be alternatives that can provide some respite. Just like Toby, therapists living in communities in crisis can feel a sense of shame for taking time out for relaxation or pleasure. They can feel worried that their clients and colleagues might judge them for taking a vacation when the situation is so challenging. Yet as Toni Morrison says in the quote earlier in this chapter, it is essential to life.

EXERCISE   Permission to Take Time Off

1. What would the critical part of you think of someone taking vacation during a crisis?

_____

_____

_____

2. What would the nurturing part of you think of someone taking vacation during a crisis?

_____

_____

_____

3. What helps you to reconcile these?

   For example, encouraging quotes, statistics about burnout and compassion fatigue, speaking with your supervisor, agreeing with a colleague, or friend to take time off at the same time and support each other, speaking with your therapist.

   Quotes such as the Toni Morrison quote above or this one from Ursula Le Guin's A Wizard of Earthsea: _"It is time you recalled that, though I am a servant, I am not your servant."_

_____

_____

_____

EXERCISE   Identifying the Need to Take Time Off

1. What are the signs that you need to take a vacation?
   - ☐ Irritable
   - ☐ Lose routine
   - ☐ Diet changes
   - ☐ Feel resentful
   - ☐ Stop doing leisure activities

☐ Home or work spaces untidy

☐ Exercise changes

☐ Stop or fall behind on administrative tasks

☐ Physical exhaustion

☐ Difficulties sleeping

☐ Increased illness

☐ Physical pain

☐ Difficulty focusing

☐ Memory issues

☐ _____

☐ _____

2. Have you noticed how many weeks you work in a row before you start to feel signs of burnout or compassion fatigue? Does that change—for better or worse—during times of crisis?

_____

3. What currently dictates how you set your amount of vacation time?

☐ Financial factors

☐ Take standard amount for my country of residence

☐ The amount that my professional body suggests

☐ The amount that my trade union suggests

☐ The same as my colleagues

☐ My organization decides

☐ Whenever I notice that I need it

☐ A set period of time, such as every 10 weeks

☐ _____

☐ _____

☐ _____

☐ _____

EXERCISE   Choosing the Right Pattern of Time Off

It can be useful to consider what amount and pattern of vacation works best for you. While you may not be able to fully implement this, it can provide you something to work toward and ensure that you are making the most of the time that you have available to take off.

1. What would be your ideal vacation pattern?
   For example, taking a week off every 7–10 weeks.

   _____

2. What are the barriers to this?

   _____

   _____

3. What could be changed to alleviate these barriers to some extent?

   _____

   _____

4. What could be an alternative or compromise?
   For example, it may be that you cannot financially afford to take more vacation but could take a week off work with clients and run workshops or training for a week instead. Like the adage goes, "a change is as good as a rest."

   _____

   _____

5. What patterns of vacation time enable you to feel most benefit?
   - ☐ One long period of time off each year
   - ☐ Taking shorter periods of time throughout the year
   - ☐ Having less vacation but taking one day or half a day off each week
   - ☐ When fewer people will also be on vacation, such as outside of school vacation
   - ☐ When my children will be on vacation from school
   - ☐ When I know my clients will be taking vacations, to reduce financial impact or to reduce difficult feelings about not being available

Rest

Dr. Saundra Dalton-Smith (2019) identifies seven types of rest: physical, mental, sensory, emotional, social, creative, and spiritual. It can be useful to identify the activities among those seven types that you enjoy and bring you a sense of rest and rejuvenation. Rest is always important. However, particularly during community and world crises, rest is imperative to your well-being. What brings a sense of rest is likely to differ from person to person and may also differ depending on a variety of personal, family, and community factors. The most important factor is to identify and practice what is right for you.

> *Jedda enjoyed spending her vacations cycling long distances on her own with just her camping gear. Being on her own outdoors brought her a great sense of peace, as did connecting with the strength of her body when she cycled. She enjoyed the creative process of mapping the routes, and she kept a journal each day, writing about and drawing what she had seen. When not on vacation, she felt most rested after a lunchtime run in the park. It helped focus her mind and gave her a break from her busy office, physically, mentally, and emotionally.*
>
> *Jedda's sister Keria thought that Jedda's vacation sounded anything but restful! Keria liked to spend her vacations with a group of her closest friends. They would hire a large house and all stay together near a beach, where they would mostly sit and chat, read or play games together. At home, Jedda felt most rested after a restorative yoga class, which involved lots of lying down in various positions while the teacher invited them to imagine beautiful scenery.*

EXERCISE Rest

1. In the table below, identify the different types of rest that are most beneficial for you. These might be the same or different when you are on vacation, on the weekends, or during a working day. There are extra empty spaces provided in case you identify additional types of rest applicable to you.

	During vacation	**Daily life**
Physical	*Example: lying on a beach; cycling long distance*	*Example: running, restorative yoga, afternoon nap*
Mental	*Example: turning off work-related notifications, playing chess*	*Example: limit news content, crossword puzzles, mindfulness*
Sensory	*Example: reducing screen time, spending time in nature*	*Example: not using phone or screens after a certain time before bed*

	During vacation	**Daily life**
Emotional	*Example: spending time with people you feel comfortable to share authentic feelings with*	*Example: going to therapy*
Social	*Example: spending time alone or with people you care about*	*Example: spending time alone or with people you care about*
Creative	*Example: visiting art galleries, reading, drawing, journaling*	*Example: basketmaking, going to a dance class, doodling*

	During vacation	Daily life
Spiritual	*Example: spending time in places that create awe and wonder*	*Example: gardening, watching birds at a feeder, religious or spiritual practices*

2. Look through the different activities you have listed in the table above. Consider which rest activities in the Daily Life column you already do through your week (daily, every other day, weekly) and which you would like to. Decide at what time and on which days you will set time aside to do these:

Day	Rest activities	Time
Monday		
Tuesday		
Wednesday		
Thursday		

Day	Rest activities	Time
Friday		
Saturday		
Sunday		

Working Time

As well as vacation, time off includes taking enough breaks in the working week. What feels like the right balance differs from person to person but also differs depending on what is going on for you and for your community.

Client numbers, hours of work, time between clients, and number of weeks between vacations are all important considerations that become even more important during times of crisis. Of course, there may need to be a practical and financial balance with these considerations too, but if your well-being suffers so that you become unable to work at all, finances will deteriorate too.

Time Inventory

Client appointments are only one aspect of the job as a therapist, but often the other parts of the role are dismissed because they are not directly generating income. This too often means that the therapist's day is so full of client appointments that all the administration tasks, even writing up session notes, get pushed into what should be time off.

Many administrative tasks do not vary with client caseload, which can mean that even when you reduce client hours, your total working hours have not reduced as much as you had expected.

1. Consider the tasks below.
2. Check any that apply to you and write the approximate number of hours or minutes you spend on this task each day, week, month. Add any additional tasks to the empty boxes.
3. If you think you might underestimate time spent, try taking note of the time actually spent during the next month.

	Minutes per day	Minutes per week	Minutes per month
☐ Client therapy planning / thinking about clients			
☐ Professional meetings and conferences			
☐ Writing case notes			
☐ Writing letters or invoices for clients			
☐ Supervision preparation			
☐ Supervision sessions			
☐ Personal therapy preparation			
☐ Personal therapy sessions			
☐ Travel to/from office			
☐ Travel to/from supervision			
☐ Travel to/from personal therapy			

	Minutes per day	Minutes per week	Minutes per month
☐ Travel to/from meetings			
☐ Continued professional development and training			
☐ Finances, accounts, taxes, insurance, and banking			
☐ Marketing and social media			
☐ Reading up-to-date literature			
☐ Housekeeping: tidying and cleaning the office, packing and unpacking resources, emptying trash, etc.			
☐ Emailing, including appointment reminders to clients			
☐ IT and website			
☐ Writing blogs, articles, research			
☐ Shopping for and buying resources			
☐ Replying to inquiries			
☐ Completing professional association–related administration			
☐ Writing reports			
☐ Initial consultations			
☐ Grounding, calming, and regulating your nervous system before, between, after clients			

4. Add up the total amount of minutes spent on administrative tasks, according to your table, per:

Day: _____

Week: _____

Month: _____

5. Consider this quote: "Work expands to fill the available time" (Parkinson, 1955). Do you have clear boundaries for your working day that include all of the tasks above? If not, what hours would you like to set for yourself each day? Fill in either or both below:

Monday: _____ to _____

Tuesday: _____ to _____

Wednesday: _____ to _____

Thursday: _____ to _____

Friday: _____ to _____

Saturday: _____ to _____

Sunday: _____ to _____

6. What is the maximum amount of time you would like to work each week?

_____

7. Looking at the amount of time spent on these tasks, consider if there is anything you wish to change about the tasks, the time spent on them, the balance with client hours, or how well held the tasks are to certain times.

For example, you may wish to delegate your financial tasks to an accountant, or to reduce the number of training sessions you attend each month, or use a program that automatically publishes pre-created posts on social media throughout the week at specified times.

	Time currently spent	Action plan	Time to spend in future
Client therapy planning/ thinking about clients			
Professional meetings and conferences			
Writing case notes			

	Time currently spent	Action plan	Time to spend in future
Writing letters or invoices for clients			
Supervision preparation			
Supervision sessions			
Personal therapy preparation			
Personal therapy sessions			
Travel to office			
Travel to supervision			
Travel to personal therapy			
Travel to meetings			
Continued professional development and training			
Tax records			
Finances, accounts, insurance, and banking			
Marketing and social media			
Reading up-to-date literature			
Housekeeping: tidying and cleaning the office, packing and unpacking resources, emptying trash, etc.			
Emailing appointment reminders to clients			
IT and website			
Writing blogs, articles, research			
Buying resources			
Replying to inquiries			

	Time currently spent	Action plan	Time to spend in future
Completing professional association–related administration			
Writing reports			
Initial consultations			
Grounding, calming, and regulating your nervous system before, between, after clients			

Adriana and her wife, Fatima, are both therapists. Adriana works in private practice and rents a therapy room by the hour, while Fatima works for a counseling service where she is employed full time.

Adriana likes to bunch all her appointments up in a morning. She has just 10 minutes between clients, to go to the bathroom and do a quick 5-minute calming activity. She rents her therapy space by the hour, which suits her financially as she doesn't need to pay room rent when she is on vacation. She also likes to have her whole afternoons free from client work. She tends to take a long lunch when she goes walking in the park with her dogs and attends a yoga class. For the rest of the afternoon, she does her administrative work and writes client notes from her home office, where she feels relaxed and comfortable.

Fatima has to be at work the whole day; there is no option for her to work from home. She only gets a 30-minute break for lunch. Though some counseling services load their therapists with clients every hour, the one Fatima works for schedules differently. Fatima is able to spread client appointments throughout the day with breaks of up to an hour in between. After each session, she cleans and tidies the room, which is necessary as she often works with creative supplies. These longer breaks enable her to spend time writing client notes right away, so that she doesn't have to carry that work around in her thoughts. She then does other administrative tasks that enable her to clear her head and focus to be fresh for the next client. For 5–15 minutes before each client appointment, she chooses a calming activity to help her feel grounded and present.

EXERCISE Time Between Sessions

Some people, like Fatima, work best with lots of time between sessions, and others, like Adriana, work better with appointments close together so that they can have a longer block of time afterward or beforehand. Some therapists write notes at the end of their workday, others following each session. Another option is to take notes during the session so it is not necessary to write them afterward.

1. Consider what daily appointment breaks work best for you. This may depend on your workplace situation and personal preference as well as the kind of therapy you offer—for example, if, like Fatima, you need time to clean and put away creative materials.
   - ☐ Appointments spaced apart with breaks in between: ideally _____ minutes apart
   - ☐ Appointments clumped together, with _____ minutes apart, to have more time before/after.
   - ☐ Appointments clumped into 3 days during the week (Monday–Wednesday, Tuesday–Thursday) to have long weekends.
2. Look at your calendar and check whether your current schedule reflects your preference.
3. What barriers stop you from having your ideal schedule?
   For example, room availability and cost, client availability, other commitments such as child care.

   _____

   _____

4. Is there anywhere in your calendar that you can get more of what you want or could do when taking on new clients?

   _____

   _____

5. What kinds of activities do you find most useful or necessary between sessions?

Fatima liked to write her client notes right away after the session so that she did not have to hold on to the material in her head.

- ☐ Bathroom break
- ☐ Calming strategies
- ☐ Write session notes
- ☐ Longer calming activities (e.g., running/yoga class) _____
- ☐ Administrative tasks
- ☐ Catch up with emails or phone calls
- ☐ Clean and tidy the space
- ☐ Get resources ready

- ☐ Other: _____
- ☐ Other: _____
- ☐ Other: _____
- ☐ Other: _____

6. After taking this time to consider your schedule, evaluate if there are any ways that you would like to change it.

   For example, would you like more time between sessions? Would you like to start using more calming strategies, work fewer days, or so on? This may be dependent on other circumstance too. When your stress levels are elevated, you may need additional time for more calming exercises than usual. Make a note of any desired changes here, along with how and when you will implement the changes.

I would like to change	I will	Date

Client Caseload

Your optimal caseload will depend on your own energy and lifestyle as well as the type of clients, type of sessions, length of sessions, what the clients are working on, what phase the client is working in, what is going on in the wider world, and so forth. There is no exact number that fits all therapists. Assessing the right balance for you can be essential to your well-being.

Jasper worked five days a week and was thinking about buying his first home. He wanted to ensure that he made enough money to be able to save for a down payment while also managing all of his professional and personal expenses. He had clients whom he had seen for many years and hadn't wanted to increase their fees too much. He decided to increase fees for old clients at the same rate as the cost of living. However, he charged new clients a more competitive rate.

If he was to reach his financial goal, Jasper realized that he needed to increase his caseload. Over the next month or so, he took on 10 new long-term clients. Not surprisingly, he found that he felt much more tired than he had expected. Then his home country, where many of his family members were still living, came under threat of war. It was an incredibly distressing time for him and he was exhausted. After a discussion with his supervisor, he initially took four weeks off. After that time, for financial reasons, he needed to return to work. When he returned to work, the situation in his home country had not stabilized, but his initial shock had decreased, and he was able to stay emotionally regulated and present with his clients. However, the large client load, which was already taking its toll before the war, felt too much. Luckily, a few of the clients he had been working with for a while came to the end of their therapy journeys, and Jasper was able to simply not replace them. In that way his caseload gradually returned to a size that was more manageable for him.

Jasper now only takes on as many clients as he feels would be manageable if he was feeling his worst. To increase his income, instead of seeing more one-to-one clients, he started to run one-time therapeutic workshops and events.

EXERCISE The Magic Number

You may already have a system to determine the number and variety of clients that works well for you. Nonetheless, it is likely that you will need to regularly review and update your balance paying attention to how it is affected by your personal responsibilities, your age, health, and physical abilities, as well as challenges in your community and the wider world.

1. Consider your current caseload:
   a. How many clients do you currently see each day? _____
   b. What is the maximum number of clients you feel you could work with on a good day? _____
   c. What is the maximum number of clients you feel you could work with on a bad day? _____
   d. Are there particular presenting issue/(s) that are "easier" for you to work with?
   e. What proportion of clients in your current caseload does this make up?
   f. Are there particular presenting issue/(s) that are more difficult for you to work with?

   _____

   g. What portion of clients in your current caseload does this make up? _____
   h. How many clients:
      • Have acute or distressing needs _____
      • Are at risk of harm or self-harm? _____
      • Have history similar to you? _____
      • Are affected by a current crisis that is also affecting you? _____
      • Are currently wishing to process trauma memories? _____
   i. Do you work better with having a caseload where:
      • Most have similar presenting issue
      • There is a wide range of presenting issues
   j. Do you find it more manageable to:
      • See lots of clients on one day and then have a day off
      • See clients spread out throughout the week
2. Looking at the information above, if you could change something about your current caseload, what would it be?
   For example, number of clients, proportion of presenting factors, proportion of long-term and short-term clients.

_____

_____

3. What could you do, short term or long term, to change this so that your caseload looks more like how you would want it to?

_____

_____

EXERCISE   Referrals and Professional Networking

No one can be a specialist in every area of trauma or therapy. As such, there will likely be clients that, because of personal preference, current gaps in your knowledge, or because the experience of the client is too triggering for you, you need to refer to another practitioner.

Having a list of practitioners who you know have a good reputation and you feel confident about recommending is essential.

1. In the space below, write the names of practitioners with their different specialties and contact information.
2. Continue to add to this list as you meet new practitioners or hear positive feedback about them.
3. Share your list with the practitioners you value and trust, and ask for their list to add to yours.
4. You might also consider proposing periodic meetings—in person or online—with your close colleagues and others from your referral list, below. That would provide possible mutual support as well as networking, and perhaps even a bit of fun.

Name	Contact	Specialty

Name	Contact	Specialty

SUPPORT NETWORK

Too often we underestimate the power of a touch, a smile, a kind word,
a listening ear, an honest compliment, or the smallest act of caring, all of
which have the potential to turn a life around. —Leo Buscaglia (1992)

Good relationships can make an incredible difference to our well-being, particularly in a crisis. Often community and world crises such as war, shootings, oppression, pandemics, contentious elections, and so on, can create rifts between people, causing many to feel less connected and more fearful of one another. Allies and support may come in many forms. You may already have a variety of support networks that you draw on for different needs.

Psychotherapists Ajay and Frank received an unexpected call from the principal at their daughter Jenna's school. They were alerted that there had been a violent incident, with injury to some of the children. Though Jenna was safe and unharmed, the principal asked them to come and get her immediately. Jenna was physically unharmed, but she had witnessed violence against her classmates and was extremely shaken up. Her parents decided to take time off to be with her. They contacted the managers at their workplaces, as well as their close family, friends, and colleagues to let them know what had happened and that though Jenna was safe and physically unhurt, she was emotionally traumatized. They also contacted their clients to let them know they would be taking two weeks off for the family emergency.

In the following days, Frank's family, who lived close by, were able to support them by cooking and bringing over meals. Most of Ajay's family lived in India, but they offered their support via videoconferencing and sent care packages.

Ajay had told his best friend, Paulo, what happened. Nonetheless, the day after the attack, Paulo had turned up for their morning run as though nothing had happened; he did not ask anything about the event, or even Jenna's or the family's welfare. Ajay felt incredibly disappointed. Speaking with his husband about this, Ajay realized that it was unlikely that his friend was indifferent and more likely that Paulo did not find speaking about emotions easy. Reflecting, Ajay realized that their friendship usually consisted of playing tennis, going for daily runs, and sharing motivational and funny stories. They rarely shared details of their emotional life. He realized that his friend continuing to show up for him each morning to motivate him to continue to exercise and have a routine had been invaluable and was Paulo's way of offering support in the only way he knew how.

Nonetheless, this highlighted a need in Ajay that was not being met by the morning runs and food deliveries. He also needed more connection and emotional support. He sent an email to the school principal and asked if she would consider setting up a support group for the parents, as well as for the children. He also found a community activist group in his area that worked in practical and supportive ways to increase well-being and reduce violent crime.

While some might have thought to immediately find therapists for the parents and for Jenna, when a trauma is recent, often good contact and support from loved ones and the community will be the best medicine and enough to mediate the effects of the trauma. Actually, long before psychotherapy and trauma therapy even existed, this is how people primarily recovered from individual and community trauma.

EXERCISE Building Your Support Network

In this exercise you will take stock of current networks and supportive communities that you already have, and consider where and how you would like to increase or expand those resources.

1. Make a list of people in your life who currently offer you support. They could be family members including animal companions, neighbors, old friends, new friends, parents of your children's friends, colleagues, community members, people at the dog park, in a spiritual or cultural community, those you have met participating in sports or classes, and so on.

   Next to each name, write the type of support you get from each person. We have made some suggestions, but you may think of other ways they offer support.

Name	Type of support
	For example, verbal or written encouragement, practical support, gift giver, makes you laugh, deep conversation, silly fun, good listener, gives good advice, motivator, shares skills and knowledge, physical affection.

2. Reading through the list above of support networks you currently have, do you notice any gaps in the type of support you would like or like more of?

3. If so, consider where you might be able to find more support. Like Ajay, you might decide to set up or find a community group. Or you might currently have a friend who you mostly get one type of support from but feel that you could build on that to extend what you offer each other.

Support type wanted	Possible places to find that support

TRAUMA-INFORMED PRACTICE

Even those of you who do not specialize in trauma therapy will likely find that many, if not most, of your clients have trauma in their history or encounter it while they are working with you. And particularly in these times, when so many countries and communities are in crisis, working with traumatized clients is inevitable for most therapists. Whether your clients are directly working on trauma issues or not, it is imperative that therapists are equipped to work in a trauma-informed way and also consider how they can be trauma-informed with their own self-care.

The impact of a traumatic event or ongoing crisis varies. What strongly affects one person may not have the same effect on another. For example, many people are deeply affected by the current ecological crisis, while others appear, at least on the surface, to mostly ignore it. How much someone is affected by living in war or under oppression is different from person to person. Some function well, some don't.

In addition to how current crises affect your client, it is important to give as much weight to how the same crises affect you. If you are currently living through an extended period of personal, world, or community trauma, it is likely that working with clients on processing their traumas could be detrimental to your own well-being. That is not a reflection on your competence, but on your humanness. If your nervous system is dysregulated because of your own trauma, it may be more difficult for you to hear details of another's trauma and experiences without it having a further dysregulating effect on you. It is important to take that into consideration as you decide what you are able to offer your clients and what you wish to focus on professionally.

EXERCISE   What Does Trauma-Informed Mean?

Trauma-informed practice will benefit both you and your client. It ensures safety and stability for your client, and also reduces the risk to you of vicarious traumatization.

At this writing, the term "trauma-informed," though used with increasing frequency, does not have a single, agreed professional definition. However, generally it includes:

- Awareness that trauma is pervasive. It can affect and impact all areas of a person's life.
- Awareness that people's behavior and presentation can be connected with a significant life-threatening event.

- Sensitivity to the emotional difficulties and possible consequences of discussing such an event, particularly with strangers.

1. Consider what the term "trauma-informed" means to you, and write your working definition below:

_____

_____

_____

2. Do you have a personal experience in therapy or the legal system that was not trauma-informed? Without describing details about the traumatic incident itself, what were the aspects that made it not trauma-informed?

For example, my supervisor insisted that my client should describe a traumatic experience to me, and then my supervisor required me to repeat the details of the experience to them.

_____

_____

_____

3. Do you have a client experience in therapy or the legal system that was not trauma-informed? Without describing details about the traumatic incident itself, what were the aspects that made it not trauma-informed?

For example, a client shared her experience of being interviewed by police after being raped. The client was asked to repeat the details of her experience over and over to different people.

_____

_____

_____

4. For the two examples you have identified above, how do you think they could have been handled in a more trauma-informed way?

For example, my supervisor could have recognized that it was premature for the client to recount their trauma and that, in addition, I was at risk of vicarious traumatization both from listening to the client's description and then being required to repeat the details to my supervisor. They could have focused on resources to help the client feel safe and stable in the present, which would have helped me as well.

*At the police station, my client could have been interviewed just once by one
or two people who were aware of how the brain and nervous system respond
in traumatic situations. If different people needed to see or hear it rather than
read the report, maybe it could have been videotaped, recorded, or witnessed
through a one-way mirror rather than making her repeat it over and over.*

_____

_____

_____

5. Are there any aspects of your professional life that you find are not trauma-
   informed and affect your ability to stay calm or think clearly?
   *For example, I am required by my workplace to ask about and make notes
   of the details of all traumatic incidents during initial interviews with all
   new clients.*

_____

_____

_____

6. Are there any steps you can take to make these areas more trauma-informed?

_____

_____

_____

EXERCISE   Principles of Trauma-Informed Therapy
and Their Application to You

In her book *The Body Remembers* (Rothschild, 2000), Babette shares 10 principles of
safe trauma therapy, given in the table below. While these are written largely in relation to the client, they may be equally applicable to the therapist.

1. Review the principles and consider how these might be applicable to you as the
   therapist. Note your thoughts in the table.

Ten principles	Applicability to therapist
First and foremost: Establish reliable safety and stabilization for the client within and outside the therapy (i.e., in the client's daily life).	*For example, I must ensure safety and stability for myself to reduce the risk of vicarious traumatization and burnout.*
Develop good contact between therapist and client as a prerequisite to applying any techniques—even if that takes months or years.	
Client and therapist must be confident in applying the "brake" before they use the "accelerator." That means the client must be in control of symptoms, including dissociation.	
Identify and build on the client's internal and external resources.	
Regard defenses as resources. Never "get rid of" coping strategies/defenses; instead, strengthen and create more choices.	
View the trauma system as a "pressure cooker." Always work to reduce—never to increase—the pressure.	
Adapt the therapy to the client, rather than expecting the client to adapt to the therapy. This requires that the therapist be familiar with several theory and treatment models.	
Have a broad knowledge of theory—both psychology and physiology of trauma and PTSD. This reduces errors and allows the therapist to create techniques tailored to a particular client's needs.	
Regard the client with their individual differences, and do not judge them for noncompliance or failure of an intervention. Never expect one intervention to have the same result with two clients.	
The therapist must be prepared, at times—or even for a whole course of therapy—to lay aside any and all techniques and just talk with the client.	

The Importance of Interruption

Retelling of trauma stories is not always useful. When the retelling is forced, premature, obsessive, more like an attempt at purging, and so on, it can actually do more harm than good. It's like a runaway train with failed breaks, nothing to slow or stop it. In addition to risks for your clients, that kind of out-of-control trauma storytelling can have a significant negative impact on your well-being, and can also hamper your ability to help your client. Risks to you include vicarious traumatization, flipping your lid, dissociation, and difficulty staying present and grounded both in and outside of the session.

Therefore, it's essential for you to be able to stop the runaway, out-of-control flood of trauma memories. The only way to do that is to, literally, interrupt your clients when they are unable to interrupt themselves. This is particularly important with clients who are living in unsafe conditions, are chronically dysregulated or dissociated, and especially when attempts at purging trauma memories becomes habitual or obsessive.

Fran's client regularly came to therapy sessions overwhelmed and was desperate to tell her trauma story. She had read that telling her story would give her catharsis and stop her from feeling so overwhelmed all the time. At each session Fran's client told all the details of being raped as a child, becoming noticeably overwhelmed and dissociated. After these sessions, despite Fran's self-care attempts, such as trying to unmirror and regulate self-talk and imagery, she nonetheless felt overwhelmed for the rest of the day. She started to have symptoms of vicarious trauma including nightmares about what she had heard and becoming jumpy when her husband touched her.

During a supervision session, Fran shared that she was in conflict about how she had been taught that therapy was supposed to be. She felt she was failing at adhering to what the client wanted and that she, the therapist, should be able to listen and handle it all. She was feeling inadequate and frozen in the sessions, as though she were trapped and unable to do anything but listen and keep trying to calm herself. Moreover, she often felt spacy and dissociated. Her supervisor reminded Fran that her key role was to facilitate the improvement of her client's day-to-day life, and that she would be unable to do that if she was overwhelmed too. They also discussed that vicarious trauma was a risk to be avoided at all costs.

The client had contracted with Fran to work on feeling more stable. However, it was clear that retelling these traumatic stories was destabilizing for both of them, and it prevented Fran from keeping her lid on so they could hold on to the therapy goal.

Fran and her supervisor strategized on how to help the client become better regulated. The best option was to interrupt the client, and help her to stabilize in that moment, so that she could learn to do the same for herself. Fran developed a plan to interrupt her client whenever she told trauma stories. She would interrupt when the client began to recount trauma and immediately direct her to use her exteroceptors to identify and name her current, present-moment, environment (I see a clock, I feel the hard cushion of the chair, I hear the dog barking outside, etc.). Fran would silently do the same to keep her own lid on.

Following a discussion of pros and cons, Fran and her client agreed that Fran would interrupt her by putting up her hand and saying "Stop" or by calling her name. Fran would then ask the client to name three things she could see in the room, in the present moment, and then three things she could hear. Fran also explained that she might need to use a louder voice than usual because when people are dysregulated or in flashback, they often can't hear very well.

At the next supervision session, Fran shared that the interrupting had helped both her and her client. At first the client had needed some time for reflection to understand that the cathartic approach, which she had been told she needed, was actually destabilizing her. Once she had realized that was true, she had readily agreed to try being interrupted. Though difficult, the client quickly felt the benefit in the session and was grateful to Fran for suggesting it. In addition, as the client got better at interrupting herself in her daily life, she noticed an improvement in her nervous system regulation and a reduction of flashbacks. As a result of the client's increased regulation through the interruption, Fran's nightmares stopped, and she was able to keep her lid on and stay present and grounded during the sessions.

We know, from the participant feedback we receive when teaching interruption in the training courses we run, that it may be uncomfortable for some of you reading this. Interrupting is frowned upon by many social cultures, as well as many approaches of psychotherapy. However, as well as protecting you from vicarious traumatization, your interruption may enable clients to get their lid back on in the moment and prevent retraumatization that too often results from the dysregulated retelling of their trauma story. We also receive feedback from training participants that once they get comfortable with it, interruption becomes a valuable addition to their skill set.

Additionally, interrupting can be useful to those of you who are not trained in or choose not to work with processing trauma memories. Not every therapist is equipped or wants to process trauma memories with their client, and it is definitely not the best option for every client. The same applies if you are supporting traumatized people as a first responder, nurse, teacher, and so on: interrupting or stopping the detailed recounting of trauma experiences will allow you to help in the ways you are trained for.

EXERCISE Pros and Cons of Interrupting Clients

1. After reading our recommendation regarding interrupting clients, notice your responses. You may have both agreeing and conflicting ideas about it. In the table below, note down the pros and cons to your well-being, regarding interrupting.

Pros to interrupting clients	Cons to interrupting clients
For example, avoiding vicarious traumatization	*For example, interrupting might have a negative effect on attunement*

2. Many therapists in our training courses agree that it is useful to interrupt clients who are increasing their overwhelm by telling their trauma story. However, some are concerned that they will be seen by their clients as rude, or as not caring about them.

    a. Make a note of any concerns you might have about interrupting.

    b. Next to that, write a way that you might overcome the problem or concern.

Concerns about interrupting	Possible solutions
For example, I am worried the client will think I am uncaring.	*For example, I know that I am interrupting because it is the most caring response; I will explain my reasons for interrupting them, at an appropriate time.*

EXERCISE   Deciding When to Interrupt

It is important to interrupt your client before they flip their lid and you flip yours. Therefore, being aware of the general indicators that they, and you, are starting to feel increased stress can be essential. Individual markers of this are also useful to note. For example, some people get a flushed face, while others get very fidgety. It might be also useful to look back over the ANS responses discussed in Chapter 3.

1. Make a list of the signs in your client that will tell you it is time to interrupt. Include general things to watch out for and other indicators of particular clients' markers of dysregulation. If you are not sure what the client is experiencing, it is wise to ask them rather than to guess, which will also help to increase their self-awareness and strengthen your partnership.
   For example, flushed or pale face, speech quickens, muscles seem tense, sweaty.

   _____

   _____

   _____

   _____

   _____

   _____

   _____

2. List the signs in yourself that will tell you that you should interrupt.
   For example, I notice my heartbeat getting faster, my foot starts twitching, my breathing feels less regular.

   _____

   _____

   _____

   _____

   _____

   _____

EXERCISE Strategize Some Ways to Talk With Your Client About Interrupting

Vanessa introduces the idea of interrupting during her initial session with clients. She gives a brief overview of how being overwhelmed is not useful to integration and how being calm is usually more useful than being overwhelmed. She checks in whether they agree that they would prefer to feel calm. Then she lets them know that sometimes when people have a difficult history, retelling traumatic stories can cause them to feel more overwhelmed.

To help them to stay calm in sessions, she lets them know that she will sometimes interrupt, not because she doesn't care about their story or that she doesn't think it is important, but to support them in being calm. Vanessa tells them that when she interrupts, she may do so quite loudly because often it is more difficult to hear during a flashback.

If there are clients you already work with, and interrupting will be new, plan to talk with them about it in a session. Like Fran, you might be nervous about how your client could react to being interrupted. Having an idea of what you'd like to say before this conversation may help increase your confidence. It may be useful to practice with a colleague or your supervisor.

1. Plan what you will say to your client about interrupting. Include why you feel it is important, and add some psychoeducation.

_____

_____

_____

2. Practice this with supervisors and colleagues and edit according to what feels right for you.

EXERCISE Strategize How You Might Interrupt

Consider some phrases and other ways that you can use to interrupt clients. These can be suggestions that you can offer your client when introducing the idea of interrupting, so that together, like Fran and her client, you can make an agreement about how you will interrupt.

1. Write some generic phrases that could be used with all clients, and consider each of your current clients and whether there would be specific ways to interrupt each.

   For example, hold up my palm; say the client's name; say, "Take a pause"; say, "Stop."

   _____

   _____

   _____

   _____

EXERCISE Make Some Plans for What to Do After the Interruption

Consider some options for exercises that you could suggest to clients to do after you have interrupted them. As described in Chapter 4, directing them to their exteroceptors is a good way to gain present-moment awareness, or asking other questions that require prefrontal cortex and awareness of the present. Discuss with your client which exteroceptor exercises are most potent for them, and experiment using them with your client to work out their preference.

For example, ask them to name three things in the room right now; ask them what today's date is; ask them what the floor feels like with their feet right now; or ask them what sounds they can hear right now.

_____

_____

_____

_____

EXERCISE Practice Interrupting

If you are unused to interrupting, it can be useful to first practice with a colleague so that you can develop confidence and normalization of the process. Practice each of the elements that have been covered in this section.

1. Ask your colleague to think of a minimally stressful event (not traumatic) from the past 24 hours (forgetting their keys, stepping in dog poop, and so on) that they could talk about in this exercise. Let them tell you a little about it, to check that it isn't too stressful for either of you, so that you can practice interrupting without either of you feeling overwhelmed.

2. Explain to your colleague why you will interrupt, using the script from the previous exercise in this section.

3. Work out together how you will interrupt, offering suggestions from the previous exercise in this section.

4. Agree upon the exercise you will direct them to after interrupting them, offering suggestions from the previous exercise in this section.

5. Ask your colleague to talk about the minimally stressful event (not traumatic) from the past 24 hours.

6. As soon as you notice signs of increased stress, even if only a little, such as speaking more quickly or slowly, looking fidgety, changes in breathing or eye contact, and so on, interrupt them.

7. Once you have interrupted them, direct them to do the activity you have agreed upon, for example, to use their exteroceptors; maybe asking them to notice what they see in the room or what sounds they can hear right now.

8. Experiment with interrupting your colleague using different tones of voice and volume. This can prepare you for the possibility that your client, when speaking quickly and engrossed in their story, or even having a flashback, would need a louder and firmer voice to interrupt.

Mildly stressful event title	For example, the store was out of my favorite flavor of chips.
Words/gesture you will use to interrupt	
Exercises you will use to direct them after interrupting	
Signs of stress in you	
Signs of stress in colleague	

Tone and volume of voice	
Comments and reflections	

EXERCISE Notice the Difference

Now that you have some experience of interrupting, it may be useful to notice the difference between when you interrupt and when you don't.

1. Ask your colleague to talk about a mildly stressful event (not traumatic) from the past 24 hours.
2. Set a timer for one minute.
3. While the colleague speaks about the stressful incident, notice your response. Maybe notice any self-talk, any imagining of the incident, any somatic responses, and changes in mood or emotion. Note any of these in the table below.
4. Next, practice the exercise above again.
5. Ask your colleague to talk about a mildly stressful event (not traumatic) from the past 24 hours. Whenever you notice signs of stress, such as speaking more quickly, or very slowly, or looking fidgety, or changes in breathing, interrupt them and direct them to their exteroceptors.
6. Again, notice your own responses during the exercise, noting them down.
7. Consider what you have noticed and whether you need to do any more practice interrupting before you start with clients.

Your response	Not interrupting	Interrupting
Somatic responses, thoughts, imagery, self-talk, mood, emotion		

EXERCISE	Evaluate Your Experience of Interrupting Your Clients

Once you have some experience of interrupting clients, reflect on how it is going: whether there have been any changes to your well-being, whether interrupting has been challenging or has gotten easier, and whether you need additional support with any aspect of interrupting.

Have you noticed any benefits to your well-being since you have been interrupting clients?	
Have you noticed any changes in your client since you have started interrupting? *For example, change in dreams or nightmares; change in ANS activation; change in behaviors*	
Have you noticed any changes in your therapeutic relationship since you started interrupting? *For example, change in attunement, change in partnership*	
What has been a challenge about interrupting?	
If something was a challenge, what support might be useful and where could you get support?	
What else have you noticed?	

CHAPTER 6

Structuring Your Own Self-Care

This chapter concludes this workbook with exercises to help you to structure and plan your self-care based on what you have learned and realized from reading and working with this book as well as other areas of your personal and professional life.

EXERCISE Review of Your Self-Care Practices

1. Take some time to go through and review the exercises in this book, including where you have noted resources that you already have.
2. Add to the sections below any exercises, activities, and resources that you feel will be useful to implement for your self-care. You may decide to add more than one to each section so that you have choice and variability depending on how you are feeling that day. And always feel free to edit and revise your plan depending on your changing needs and circumstances.
3. Add them to your calendar so that they become valued tasks during your day.
4. Consider how and over what time period you will assess their value and whether you want to swap in other exercises for those that are not working for you now or anymore.
5. Notice if they are useful at particular places and times and less useful at other times.

Self-care practices before work	If useful, in what way? (e.g., feel calm, energized, competent)	In what place/ time is it most useful?

Self-care practices before each client appointment	If useful, in what way? (e.g., feel calm, energized, competent)	In what place/ time is it most useful?

Self-care practices between each client appointment	If useful, in what way? (e.g., feel calm, energized, competent)	In what place/time is it most useful?

Self-care practices after each client appointment	If useful, in what way? (e.g., feel calm, energized, competent)	In what place/time is it most useful?

Self-care practices at the end of the work day	If useful, in what way? (e.g., feel calm, energized, competent)	In what place/ time is it most useful?

Self-care practices specific to particular clients/presenting issues	Client initials	If useful, in what way? (e.g., feel calm, energized, competent)

Other self-care practices to implement	Day/time	If useful, in what way? (e.g., feel calm, energized, competent)	In what place/ time is it most useful?

EXERCISE Review of Your Resources

In Chapter 1, you took an inventory of your current resources. Some of those might be things that you do or call on regularly, irregularly, or that you have noticed have been useful in the past but are not currently in your routine.

1. In the table below, read through the resource suggestions and add any that appeal to you.
2. Reflect on the past two weeks and check any that you are already doing. Evaluate their usefulness.
3. Next, check any that you would like to start or restart doing.
4. In the comments section, write what this will look like. Be realistic!
5. For example, if eating healthily is something that you would like to do more of, you might decide to start by making a healthy packed lunch for work every Wednesday.
6. If financial savings is something you would like to start but are currently struggling

with, you could decide to save a couple of dollars per week for now to get in the habit.

7. Continue to assess their usefulness each week: Not useful = 0 to Very useful = 10

8. If you notice something is no longer useful, consider why that might be and whether it would be more helpful for you to adapt it or to switch it out for something different.

✔	Resource	Comments/plan	Usefulness Not useful = 0 to Very useful = 10
	Example: Exercise	*Walk to work on a Thursday when my partner can take the kids to school.*	*8*
Practical resources			
	Regularly serviced car		
	Have or working toward financial stability and savings		
	Carry a personal alarm		
Physical resources			
	Eat healthily		
	Exercise		
	Regular medical and dental check-ups		
	Getting enough sleep		

✔	Resource	Comments/plan	Usefulness Not useful = 0 to Very useful = 10
	Making time to rest		
	Massage or physical therapy		
	Take vitamins or supplements if necessary		
	Sex or pleasurable touch		
Interpersonal resources			
	Get to know and spend time with my neighbors		
	Spend time with people I love or care about		
	Part of a community/ advocacy group		
	Part of an activity group/ class		
	Peer supervision		

✔	Resource	Comments/plan	Usefulness Not useful = 0 to Very useful = 10
Psychological resources			
	Mindfulness		
	Personal therapy sessions		
	Journaling		
	Reading for enjoyment		
	Watch movies		
	Advocate for yourself or your community		
	Spend time with animal companions		
Spiritual resources			
	Yoga class		
	Sitting or walking in nature		
	Going to a place of worship		

✔	Resource	Comments/plan	Usefulness Not useful = 0 to Very useful = 10
	Listen to music		
	Gardening/growing food or flowers		
	Watching birds		
	Meditation		
Other resources			

EXERCISE Barriers to Self-Care

It can be useful to plan ahead for what might stop you from taking action and making changes, so that you can be prepared and plan ways to support yourself.

1. What barriers to self-care do you predict will make it difficult to carry out your self-care plan?

   For example, getting my children to school in the morning prevents me from going to a morning yoga class that I feel would be beneficial.

2. How can you get support with these barriers?

   For example, I will arrange with another parent friend at the school to take turns taking each other's children to school so that every other day I can go to my morning yoga class.

Barrier	Support
Example: Getting my children to school in the morning prevents me from getting to a morning yoga class that I feel would be beneficial.	*Example: I will arrange with another parent friend at the school to take turns taking each other's children to school so that every other day I can go to my morning yoga class.*

EXERCISE Small Steps

In this exercise, you will make lists of strategies most useful for you and plans of what to do before sessions, during sessions, and after sessions with clients. For some of you, implementing everything at once, diving right in at the deep end, will feel right for you; for others that will feel overwhelming.

It can be daunting to make changes to your life, particularly when faced with lots of options. One way to avoid the feeling of being overwhelmed is to make the changes in very small steps, just adding one thing at a time to your usual routine.

1. After reading this book, is there something that stood out to you as being particularly useful or important to you to change or add to your self-care?

_____

_____

2. Is there something that would be small enough to add (or that you could add a small portion of) to your current routine without any feeling of stress or anxiety?

3. If not, could you break it down into smaller steps to make it more manageable? *For example, go for a 20-minute walk every day at lunchtime.*
   - Step 1: Look at my calendar to work out what time is best for me.
   - Step 2: If necessary, arrange for new time with clients to accommodate my walk.
   - Step 3: Put "lunchtime walk" into calendar as a reminder on the day and the day before so I remember to take my walking shoes and coat.
   - Step 4: Plan a route that I will enjoy.
   - Step 5: Decide to go for a shorter walk, and work out a good amount of time, if the full route feels in any way daunting to me.
   - Step 6: Ask if any colleagues or friends would like to join me for motivation.

4. There may be small steps to actually going on the walk too, if that also feels in any way daunting, such as:
   - Step 1: Change my shoes.
   - Step 2: Put on my coat.
   - Step 3: Go out of the door . . . and so on.

5. Self-care change:

_____

   - Step 1: _____
   - Step 2: _____
   - Step 3: _____
   - Step 4: _____
   - Step 5: _____
   - Step 6: _____

6. Consider the resources outside work and the self-care at work you'd like to develop, and notice which are possible to easily add to your routine.

Today: _____

Resources I need to be able to do this: _____

_____

Tomorrow: _____

Resources I need to be able to do this: _____

_____

Next week: _____

Resources I need to be able to do this: _____

_____

EXERCISE   Reconnect With Your Values and Drive

Reconnecting with our values and our purpose in our work can often help to give a greater sense of grounding.

> *Robyn worked in a busy charity with lots of paperwork, deadlines to meet, and short-term, time-limited clients to meet the requirements of funding. She felt overwhelmed and exhausted with work and, due to the low wage, was not able to save to go on vacation or to put money into a pension. The work felt never-ending.*
>
> *When she took the job, her plan had been to work for the charity part-time, and to start to build a private practice part-time. She had wanted to give time to a charity that was important to her values, but to balance that with a private practice, where she would have more choice of working hours, types of difficulties, and better income. That would enable her to save a pension and to save money to complete supervision training to give more diversity to her working week.*
>
> *However, with the high demands of that job and the initial passion for the charity work, her original plan had been forgotten. Robyn had begun to feel fed up with the job in general, overwhelmed by the hours and bureaucracy. After a particularly tricky day, Robyn's wife mentioned that she had seen some office space to rent that might be good for private practice, and this reminded her of the original plan. That weekend they went to a party, and a new friend of Robyn's*

wife asked her what had inspired her to become a psychotherapist. Robyn paused for a moment, and found she had to think hard about the answer.

The next day, Robyn took some time to really consider that question and to journal her answers. She considered her values, what she saw the purpose of her work to be, what was important to her about the work, what particular areas and memories made her feel proud or enlivened, and what her new plan was.

She rewrote these out and stuck them on her desk so that she would see them every day and started to consider the small steps needed to get balance to her work. Her purpose renewed, and with a clear path, she felt much less defeated, overwhelmed, and burnt out. A few weeks later, she agreed with her boss on a new part-time rota and enrolled on a supervision training course.

1. Thinking back, what drew you to becoming a helping professional?

_____

_____

_____

_____

2. What do you enjoy about your work as a helping professional?

_____

_____

_____

_____

3. Is there a particular memory or memories that you have where you felt proud of what you do? Describe it below.

_____

_____

_____

_____

4. Are you satisfied with where you are and where you are going in your career? Are you content with what you are doing now, or do you envisage doing anything differently in the future? When do you think you will retire? Do you plan

to take any additional training to diversify what you do? Do you want to vary your schedule to include work that is not connected with therapy? For example, Babette always preferred to have some of her working hours be non-client related. She had different part-time jobs before she started teaching and writing books. Vanessa works as a psychotherapist, a basket maker, yoga teacher, and mountain guide.

_____

_____

_____

_____

5. Considering what you have written above, is there anything you would need to put into place to feel more satisfied with your work or future work?
   For example, start supervision training, stop taking on new clients to have more time for other work interests.

_____

_____

_____

_____

6. How will you maintain awareness of your values, purpose and path? Like Robyn, you might write them out and display them somewhere you will see them often, or decide on some tasks to help you to start any new ventures or ways of working.

_____

_____

_____

_____

Support for Your Self-Care

Robyn's wife and wife's friend had both encouraged Robyn to reconsider her working circumstances, which inspired her to make changes that significantly improved her well-being. It was also a good learning experience for Robyn as she realized that she might have avoided overwhelm and burnout if she had asked someone to support her sooner.

Similarly, when Vanessa started a new exercise plan, she invited some friends to join her. Not only would that make it more fun, but they could also hold each other accountable. It was useful to all members of the group.

Asking a friend, colleague, supervisor, or even creating a self-care support network can enable you to feel motivated and accountable for your self-care and enable you to offer that for someone else at the same time.

1. Ask one or more people to support your self-care plan. It can be a family member, friend, colleague, coach, mentor, whomever. List the people you think might be good candidates here:

   _____

   _____

   _____

2. Before speaking to them, consider your needs, so that you can be explicit about what you are asking for and more likely to get what you need. For example:
   • How would you prefer them to help you to keep going with your self-care?

   _____

   • How often and what method would you prefer them to check in with you?

   _____

   • Would you be open to this being mutual, doing the same for them?

   _____

3. When you ask for support, be sure to be clear about your needs and whether they are able to meet them or if there needs to be a compromise. Also, if you decide on mutual support, check the best way for you to support them with their self-care.

CONCLUSION

We hope that this workbook will be an ongoing guide, source, and support for continuing your own personal and professional self-care. Our advice is to stay vigilant, as it is so easy for a commitment to one's self-care to slip down the priority list.

Checking in frequently with yourself—or even better, checking in with a supportive colleague group that shares self-care goals—will ensure that you continue to be able to engage in the work you love. Frequently revisit your goals and the tools that help you reach them. Freely revise as your personal and professional situation changes and evolves. Consider that doing so will also allow you to be a role model for your clients, colleagues, and supervisees. Just about everyone struggles with self-care, but it is contagious. Taking care of you has the potential to inspire others to do the same.

Of course life has inevitable ups and downs that will impact your self-care. Sometimes you will need extra support, sometimes less, and (like all of us) you will sometimes forget to take care of yourself altogether. Make sure you notice and accept all of these variations with compassion towards yourself. *Always* be on your side.

Feel free to contact us with questions or to make suggestions for future editions and more books. We welcome your feedback!

References

Bear, V. (2024). *Wild & well-being card deck: 70 exercises for nature-based self care*. Norton.

Bolmont, B., Gangloff, P., Vouriot, A., & Perrin, P. (2002) Mood states and anxiety influence abilities to maintain balance control in healthy human subjects. *Neuroscience Letters, 329*(1), 96–100.

Brown, D. (Writer & Presenter). (2007, April 13). Trick or treat [TV series episode]. In A. O'Connor (Executive Producer), Derren Brown: Trick or treat. Objective Productions; Channel 4 Television.

Buscaglia, L. (1992). *Born for love: Reflections on loving*. Slack Incorporated.

Callaway, J. (Host). (1977). Born this day: Toni Morrison in conversation with John Callaway [TV broadcast]. WTTW Television.

Crego, A., Yela, J. R., Riesco-Matías, P., Gómez-Martínez, M. Á., & Vicente-Arruebarrena, A. (2022). The benefits of self-compassion in mental health professionals: A systematic review of empirical research. *Psychology Research and Behavior Management, 15*, 2599–2620.

Damasio, A. R. (1994). *Descartes' error: Emotion reason, and the human brain*. Avon Books.

Damasio, A. R. (1999). *The feeling of what happens: Body and emotion in the making of consciousness*. Harcourt Brace.

Dalton-Smith, S. (2019) *Sacred rest: Recover your life, renew your energy, restore your sanity*. Faith Words.

Ekman, P. (1972). Universal and cultural differences in facial expression of emotions. In J. Cole (Ed.), Nebraska Symposium on Motivation (pp. 207–283). Lincoln: University of Nebraska Press.

Ekman, P., Levenson, R. W., & Friesen, W. V. (1983). Autonomic nervous system activity distinguishes among emotions. *Science*, 221, 1208–1210.

Figley, C. R. (2002). Compassion fatigue: Psychotherapists' chronic lack of self care. *Journal of Clinical Psychology, 58*(11), 1433–1441.

Gallese, V., Eagle, M. N., & Migone, P. (2007). Intentional attunement: mirror neurons and the neural underpinnings of interpersonal relations. *Journal of the American Psychoanalytic Association, 55*(1), 131–176.

Kohut, H. (1971). *The analysis of the self: A systematic approach to the psychoanalytic treatment of narcissistic personality disorders*. International Universities Press.

MacLean, P. D. (1985). Brain evolution relating to family, play, and the separation call. *Archives of General Psychiatry, 42*(4), 405–417.

Maslach, C., Leiter, M. P. (1997). *The truth about burnout: How organizations cause personal stress and what to do about it.* Jossey-Bass/Wiley

Merriam-Webster. (2024). compassion. https://www.merriam-webster.com/dictionary/compassion.

Miller, K., & Kelly, A. (2020). Is self-compassion contagious? An examination of whether hearing a display of self-compassion impacts self-compassion in the listener. *Canadian Journal of Behavioral Science/Revue canadienne des sciences du behavior, 52*(2), 159.

Parkinson, C. N. (1955, November 19). Parkinson's Law. *The Economist.*

Rajagopalan, A., Jinu, K. V., Sailesh, K. S., Mishra, S., Reddy, U. K., & Mukkadan, J. K. (2017). Understanding the links between vestibular and limbic systems regulating emotions. *Journal of Natural Science, Biology and Medicine, 8*(1), 11–15.

Richardson, C. M., Trusty, W. T., & George, K. A. (2020). Trainee wellness: Self-critical perfectionism, self-compassion, depression, and burnout among doctoral trainees in psychology. *Counselling Psychology Quarterly, 33*(2), 187–198.

Rothschild, B. (2000). *The body remembers: The psychophysiology of trauma and trauma treatment.* Norton.

Rothschild, B. (2010). *8 keys to safe trauma recovery: Take-charge strategies to empower your healing* (8 Keys to Mental Health). Norton.

Rothschild, B. (2017) *Autonomic nervous system table.* Norton.

Rothschild, B. (2021) *Revolutionizing trauma treatment: Stabilization, safety, & nervous system balance.* Norton.

Rothschild, B. (2022). *Help for the helper: Preventing compassion fatigue and vicarious trauma in an ever-changing world: Updated + expanded* (2nd ed.). Norton.

Rothschild, B., Bear, V. (2023). *8 keys to safe trauma recovery workbook* (8 Keys to Mental Health). Norton.

Schroeder, E. (2014). Elke Schroeder [website]. Retrieved Oct 28, 2024, from https://www.elkebschroeder.com/teaching

Siegel, D. (2010). *The mindful therapist: A clinician's guide to mindsight and neural integration.* Norton.

Sissay, L. (2024). *Let the light pour in.* Canongate Books.

Stel, M., van den Heuvel, C., & Smeets, R. C. (2008). Facial feedback mechanisms in autistic spectrum disorders. *Journal of Autism and Developmental Disorders, 38,* 1250–1258.

Stern, D. (1985). *The interpersonal world of the infant: A view from psychoanalysis and developmental psychology.* Basic Books.

Strack, F., Martin, L. L., & Stepper, S. (1988). Inhibiting and facilitating conditions of the human smile: A nonobtrusive test of the facial feedback hypothesis. *Journal of Personality and Social Psychology, 54*(5), 768–777. https://doi.org/10.1037/0022-3514.54.5.768

Substance Abuse and Mental Health Services Administration. (2014). SAMHSA's Concept of Trauma and Guidance for a Trauma-Informed Approach. HHS Publication No. (SMA) 14-4884. Substance Abuse and Mental Health Services Administration.

Tzu, L. (1996). *Tao te ching* (A. Waley, Trans.). Wordsworth Editions.

Yirmiya, N., Sigman, M., Kasari, C., & Mundy, P. (1992). Empathy and cognition in high functioning children with autism. *Child Development, 63*, 150–160.

Index

Note: Italicized page locators refer to figures; tables are noted with a *t*.

About the Authors

Babette Rothschild, MSW, has been a practitioner since 1976 and a teacher and trainer since 1992. She is the author of seven books, (translated into more than 19 languages including Arabic, Danish, German, French, Spanish, and Japanese) all published by Norton, including her bestseller, *The Body Remembers: The Psychophysiology of Trauma and Trauma Treatment* (2000), as well as *Revolutionizing Trauma Treatment: Stabilization, Safety, & Nervous System Balance* (2017, 2021). She is also the series editor of Norton's 8 Keys to Mental Health series. After living and working for nine years in Copenhagen, Denmark in the 1990s, she returned to her native Los Angeles. There she writes while continuing to lecture, train, and supervise professional psychotherapists worldwide. In recent years, together with members of her Somatic Trauma Therapy team, Norton's London office, the Complex Trauma Institute, and Doctors Without Borders, she has been active in providing pro bono training and support for thousands of psychotherapists and helping professionals in Ukraine and other crisis areas around the world. For more information, visit her website at www.trauma.cc.

Vanessa Bear, MSc, UKCP reg, is a psychotherapist, clinical supervisor (in training), educator, and author whose work centers on sustainable well-being for therapists. She specializes in embodied, nature-connected, and creative approaches to practitioner self-care, translating psychological ideas into clear, accessible tools for everyday clinical practice. She is the coauthor of *8 Keys to Safe Trauma Recovery Workbook* (2023) and the author of the *Wild and Well-Being Card Deck* (2024), both published by Norton.

Vanessa delivers workshops and guest lectures across the UK, both online and in person, on self-care for helping professionals. Her teaching integrates eco-psychotherapy, yoga, mindfulness, and trauma-informed approaches to support regulation, resilience, and reflective practice. A certified Somatic Trauma Therapist, she also assists on Somatic Trauma Therapy trainings with Babette Rothschild. Her work is grounded in supporting therapists to care for themselves with safety, clarity, compassion, and professional sustainability. Find resources at wildandwellbeing.com.